WRITE MAGIC SYSTEMS YOUR READERS WON'T FORGET

A TOOLKIT
FOR FICTION WRITERS

STANT LITORE

Westmarch Publishing | 2022

MORE FROM STANT LITORE

THE DAKOTARAPTOR RIDERS

Gladiators
Incursion

THE ZOMBIE BIBLE

Death Has Come up into Our Windows
What Our Eyes Have Witnessed
Strangers in the Land
No Lasting Burial
I Will Hold My Death Close
By a Slender Thread (forthcoming)

OTHER TITLES

Ansible: A Thousand Faces
Dante's Heart

The Dark Need (The Dead Man #20)
with Lee Goldberg, William Rabkin

&

Lives of Unforgetting
Lives of Unstoppable Hope
On the Other Side of the Night
Write Characters Your Readers Won't Forget
Write Worlds Your Readers Won't Forget
Write Stories Your Readers Won't Forget
Write Descriptions Your Readers Won't Forget
0 to 60: Write Pacing Your Readers Won't Forget
Beat Writer's Block and Reignite Your Creativity

Write Magic Systems Your Readers Won't Forget

STANT LITORE

WESTMARCH PUBLISHING

2022

ISBN 978-1-7362127-8-3

You can reach Stant Litore at:
www.stantlitore.com
www.patreon.com/stantlitore
zombiebible@gmail.com

CONTENTS

for Y, who will be delighted by this book

1 | WRITING MAGIC

BECAUSE YOU ARE READING THIS BOOK, it's likely that you've found magic exciting in stories you've read or seen, perhaps since you were a small child, and now you want to write a story in which magic exists. And you want to do it well. *Write Magic Systems Your Readers Won't Forget* will help you create the framework for what magic is doing in your story, why it matters to your characters, and how it works—and it will help you think more creatively and boldly about the storytelling possibilities your magic system opens up for you. After all, that's what magic is all about: imagining and enacting unexpected possibilities. There will be a delicious tension throughout this book between our excitement at the wildness and unpredictability of magic and our desire for a magic *system* (by which we usually mean a set of rules, conditions, or explanations that permit the writer to use magic in the story in a way that is compelling and consistent and that permits the reader to "follow" what's going on). This tension is both necessary and ok; it's the very tension that is at work in any act of storytelling and in any process of learning the storytelling craft. It is the tension between play and rigor, and between creativity and structure. After all, storycraft is one of the original forms of spellcraft; it is an arcane yet ever-evolving art by which we use words to conjure things from that otherworld of the imagination into a brief and vivid existence in the minds of our readers. Fiction is magic.

In this book, we will discuss the four things you may want to get specific about in order to devise a magic system for a work of fiction: the *costs, cultural function, mechanics*, and *ethics* of magic. At the end of the book (see Chapter 6, Exercise 32), you will find a worksheet for the design of a magic system; if you would find it useful to do so, as you complete the exercises in this book, I invite you to jot down your notes in that worksheet (or in your own notebook, using that worksheet as a guide).

But before delving into questions of technique, I want to start by emphasizing what drives us to want a magic system in our story in the first place. Why magic? Because magic interrupts the steady, mundane flow of cause and effect, introducing the unexpected and the wildly playful. It is one means by which a writer tosses something new into the world of their story, like a rock thrown into a pond, sending out ripples or waves and making our characters' lives dance, like little paper boats, on the turbulence.

OUR FIRST SCENT OF MAGIC

Consider this. How will you introduce the magic in your story to the reader? To do so *unforgettably*, think first not about how magic works (we will get there shortly) but about what magic *means*—how it affects the lives of the people it touches, and how they feel about it. In other words, *what should the effect of your magic be on your characters, and on the reader?* For example, here is how Robin McKinley opens her novel *Spindle's End*, and it's one of the most unforgettable narrative openings I have ever read. Watch what she does:

> The magic in that country was so thick and tenacious that it settled over the land like chalk-dust and over floors and shelves like slightly sticky plaster-dust. (Housecleaners in that country earned unusually good wages.) If you lived in that country, you had to de-scale your kettle of its encrustation of magic at least once a week, because if you didn't, you might find yourself pouring hissing snakes or pond slime into your teapot instead of water...
>
> People either loved that country and couldn't imagine living anywhere else, or hated it, left it as soon as they could, and never came back. If you loved it, you loved coming over the last hill before your village one day in early autumn and hearing the cornfield singing madrigals, and that day became a story you told your grandchildren, the way in other countries other grandparents told the story of the day they won the betting pool at the pub, or their applecake won first place at the local fete. If you lived there, you learned what you had to do, like putting a pinch of dried dja vine in your kettle once a week, like asking your loaf of bread to remain a loaf of bread before you struck it with a knife. The people of this country had developed a reputation among outsiders for being unusually pious, because of the number of things they appeared to mutter a blessing over before they did them; but in most cases this was merely the asking of things it was safer to ask to remain nonmagical first, while work or play or food preparation or

whatever was being got on with. Nobody had ever heard of a loaf of bread turning into a flock of starlings for anyone they knew, but the nursery tale was well known, and in that country it didn't pay to take chances.

ROBIN MCKINLEY, *SPINDLE'S END*

Magic in *Spindle's End* is simultaneously *wonder* and *nuisance*, and as readers, we have never encountered magic in quite this way before. This magic is so everyday that household chores are adapted to cope with it, yet also so unpredictable and strange that it has lost none of its marvel. Encountering magic as something that has to be scrubbed off a platter to prevent the resurrection of your Thanksgiving turkey or your chicken dumplings is truly unforgettable!

Here's how Alice Hoffman speaks of magic, at the end of her novel *Practical Magic*:

> By the time she runs down the bluestone path, it doesn't make a bit of difference what people think or what they believe. There are some things, after all, that Sally Owens knows for certain: Always throw spilled salt over your left shoulder. Keep rosemary by your garden gate. Add pepper to your mashed potatoes. Plant roses and lavender, for luck. Fall in love whenever you can.

ALICE HOFFMAN, *PRACTICAL MAGIC*

In both cases—*Practical Magic* and *Spindle's End*—"magic" is the unexpected factor that enters our experience, with the potential to upend our day or even transform our life.

It's as marvelously unpredictable as one's pie bursting into a flock of snails, or as unexpected as falling in love.

The more we talk in this book about creating a magic *system*, the more important it is to remember that magic, even when it can be studied, worked, or wielded, even when it's *practical*, is nevertheless the wild element, the unpredictable, the eruption of the seemingly impossible into our ordinary world. That is not to say that magic in a fictional world has to be inherently unnatural. It *might* be unnatural. Or, within your imagined world, it might be the most *natural* thing there is—perhaps even an emanation of life itself, something that life produces or emits, like the Force in *Star Wars*. Yet what could be stranger, less predictable or more wild, than life? It is the nature both of life and of magic to resist our control, to defy our attempts to define, restrict, and manipulate. "Life finds a way," mathematician Ian Malcom remarks in Steven Spielberg's film adaptation of *Jurassic Park*. So does magic—particularly when wielded by the unwary or the underprepared. In Disney's *Fantasia*, Mickey Mouse might put on a wizard's hat and set a broom to doing his housework, but once he has set the broom in motion, will it ever stop? Can he predict what that first act of epic sweepery will lead to? Even the wary and the wise may find magic difficult to manage. In *The Lord of the Rings*, Gandalf the wizard has a devil of a time figuring out the password that, once spoken, will open a secret door, and the One Ring itself (the most powerful magical device in that fictional world) has a way of slipping off one's finger and rolling away all on its own, making its escape when you aren't looking.

So, before we map out how magic *works*, what it costs, or what effects it has, the first step is to consider what magic *means* and how you might go about evoking it in a story. To consider this, explore how *you* feel about the unpredictable nature of life, about the unexpected, about the strange and the uncanny. How would *you* respond if a hundred brooms swept into your home carrying pails of water, or if your delicious, home-baked pie burst abruptly into a flock of snails, or if tomorrow, indeed, tomorrow morning, an hour after dawn, you were to fall deliciously, surprisingly, impossibly in love? Imagine the answer to that, and you'll know better what magic means to you and how to write it.

Take a few moments and ponder that. Once you have jotted down some notes, come back to this page, and we'll take a brief look at these three questions that you can explore for your story:

1. What is magic like?
2. What are magic users like?
3. What do magic users believe about their magic?

1. WHAT IS MAGIC LIKE?

In *Practical Magic* and in *Spindle's End*, magic exists in a specific relationship to the world. Find that relationship, and you will find the foundation for the magic system you will create. Your magic system will articulate, express, and define or imply the parameters of that relationship, just as wedding vows or a prenuptial agreement articulate a marriage, a constitution and law articulate a state, and a creed and rites articulate an orthodoxy.

So what is that relationship? What is magic like? How would *you* introduce magic to the reader? And what will that introduction imply about what magic *means* to your characters and to their fictional world?

Exercise 1

What is the first act of magic your readers will see? You might consider what spell or wonder would be most surprising and entertaining for your readers. Or, you might consider which would propel your protagonist speedily into the story. Consider what kind of story you're trying to tell. If it's a "sorceror's apprentice" story, in which a young magic worker's spellcraft goes hilariously or tragically awry at the start, then it's a matter of thinking through what might be most entertainingly absurd or shockingly horrific, or perhaps what might get your character into trouble with a parent, a village, or a school principal. In the first pages of Ursula K. LeGuin's *A Wizard of Earthsea*, young Ged tries to charm and command a herd of goats, but the goats become so enamored with him that they won't let him be; he ends up walking slowly back to his village with a ring of devoted goats enclosing him!

Or perhaps your characters are just trying to quietly live their lives in some pleasant shire or out-of-the-way corner of the world, and magic injects a note of strangeness and unease into their bucolic setting; in J.R.R. Tolkien's *The Fellowship of the Ring*, our first outburst of magic involves an eccentric old hobbit turning abruptly invisible and vanishing from a birthday party, leaving his guests astounded and appalled. In the scene that follows, we begin to suspect that Bilbo's invisibility ring is having an uneasy effect on his mind and character.

Or maybe your story requires, instead, *immediate danger* at the outset; Max Gladstone's novel *Three Parts Dead* opens with Tara Abernathy ejected from a school for young witches and shoved out of a door in the sky to plummet through thousands of feet of empty air; her first spell is a desperate attempt to slow her fall. So, consider what kind of story you are trying to tell and what kind of introduction the reader needs to that story—what mood and effect those first pages need to create. The first appearance of magic in your story can be crafted to help create that effect.

Another way to brainstorm your reader's first encounter with magic is to approach it through sensory detail. For example, you could ask yourself: What does magic *smell* like? Do some acts of magic smell like honey mead or a sea breeze? Do some acts of magic smell like decay, like the corpse of a cat found in the alley with maggots writhing beneath its skin? Does some magic smell like burned toast, and other magic like roses? Perhaps you can even open your story with your character encountering an unexpected scent, taste, or sound, a sensory prelude to the magic that is about to erupt onto the page. Does magic sound like a distant melody that you can't quite make out but can't ignore either (as in Susan Cooper's *The Dark is Rising*), or does magic sound like a distant, eerie screech, nails on a chalkboard as large as the sky but half a planet away? Write a paragraph in which a character smells, tastes, or hears *magic*, and explore the impact this sensory experience has on your character's emotions.

Exercise 2

Considering what you wrote in Exercise 1, complete the following sentence:

Magic is a _____.

Is it a *tool*? Is it a *language*? Is it both? What do you think the function of magic may be, in your story-world? Does it solve problems? Does it create problems? Is it a nuisance, as in *Spindle's End*? Or a spice, a flavor, a brilliance added to our lives, like love, like rosemary, as in *Practical Magic*? Write a sentence about what magic *is* and what it's *like*, and then keep testing that sentence (or adding *if*s, *and*s, *but*s, and provisos as needed) while you continue to develop your story.

2. WHAT ARE MAGIC USERS LIKE?

Exercise 3

Now complete the following sentence:

Magic users are _____.

If magic is a nuisance, are mages the cleanup crew? Or are they the tricksters, pickpockets, and unrepentant 'trolls' of your world? If magic is a spice, a flavor, a dash of light and color and music in our lives, are mages then the chefs, the culinary artisans, the skilled (hopefully) wonder-workers who know when to add just a pinch of ginger, and who also know when more than a pinch is too much?

"Meddle not in the affairs of wizards, for they are subtle and quick to anger"—that is Gildor the elflord's advice, in J.R.R. Tolkien's *The Fellowship of the Ring*. And such advice—whether it be good or no—brings us to an alternative entry point to discussing the role of magic in your fictional story. In the preceding pages, we've been talking about the *wildness* of magic, the element of chaos or wonder that it might bring into your characters' daily lives. Now let's consider the *humanity* of magic users. What makes mages grouchy and quick to anger? What makes them subtle or overt? What makes them impassioned? What makes them tired? What makes them noble? How do magic users see themselves?

Are there gradations among the mages in your world? Are there some tricksters who make roses sprout from a liar's mouth whenever he speaks—using their magic to provide a perverse but poetic justice—while there are others whose pranks are malevolent and destructive and terrible in their impact, mages who make nuclear missiles arm themselves and explode on their own, or who turn candles into forest fires?

Are there disagreements between the mages in your world? If the magic workers are the world's *chefs*, does one think a given situation requires only a "pinch" of magic (like a pinch of garlic), while another thinks you can never have too much, an entire clove is needed, at least? Does one mage merely sweeten the wine at a wedding, or add magical blush to the bride's cheeks, while another transforms the guests into lions and makes sudden elephants tapdance on the tables, and makes a tree of the most succulent, juicy, and aphrodisiac fruit sprout from the wedding cake, as unexpectedly as love at first sight and as delicious as true love itself?

Is there a mage who simply can't stand another's work? Consider this conversation from a post on tumblr, on the topic of *how to write a character who is an expert*:

HOMUNCULUS-ARGUMENT: Hey, to you sci-fi/fantasy writers out there (and maybe some others, but this is mainly for things that *can't* really be researched irl), if you want to write a character who is a driven, passionate expert on something, don't write about them rambling indifferently about some boring, mundane part of it. Give them a deep, intense hatred of some oddly specific wow-i-did-not-even-know-that-was-a-thing-and-it-would-have-never-occurred-to-me-that-it's-a-*bad*-thing thing they'll gladly rant about.

Write a dragon rider who really fucking hates it when a dragon is trained to bow while being reined. A space ship engineer who is pissed off when [a] perfectly good antimatter ship has been adapted to run on neutral matter. A historian who is *still* not over the massive failures of a general who lost a specific battle 300 years before she was born.

The guy currently giving us a series of lectures on the restoration of historical buildings really, *really* hates polymer paint. At the artisan school our stained glass teacher really hated this one specific Belgian artist—we never really figured out what did that guy even *do*, but he's been dead for over 200 years and our teacher was glad that at least he's dead.

Experts don't just *know* things you've never thought about. They've got strong opinions about it.

DERINTHESCARLETPESCATARIAN: This is a great way to not only make your experts more realistic and give them personality and lively rivalries, but a great way to sneak some exposition in. It's important for your readers to know how the fuel in your spaceship is refined but there's no way to sneak it in without it sounding like a lecture? Give your fuel tech *very strong opinions* on it and have a running gag where any time someone mentions fuel, they immediately have to start trying to shut him up.

MALUS-SYL-VESTRIS: If you want realistic biologists, let them argue passionately about taxonomic classification. Biologists have *opinions* about taxonomic classification and discovering alien life is guaranteed to bring even more opinions to the field so...

ALLTHINGSLINGUISTIC: Also, the more someone has expertise in a particular area, the more *painfully* they're aware of all the slightly adjacent areas they don't have expertise in and exactly who does. I'm tired of fictional linguists who know all the things about all the languages, give me more linguists who are like "hmm, looks like Proto-Alpha-Centaurian, probably from the 28th century, which I don't know anything about really, but I did meet this linguist who works on it back when I was a grad student and we get coffee every year at the galactic conference and you know, I disagree with their entire theoretical approach but their data is very solid and they're very supportive of their students, here's their contact info, you can tell 'em I sent ya."

What scholarly pet peeve sends *your* magical expert off on a rant—or guarantees they will get involved and enter the fray? In the film *Stargate*, the archaeologist Daniel, who may not be particularly inclined to adventure, gets completely hooked when he finds a translation from ancient Kemetic (Egyptian) on a chalkboard; he is so irritated at the ineptness of the translation (*"Why* are people still reading Budge's work?!") that he re-translates it on the spot; the inscription concerns a Stargate, and following his infuriated demonstration of expertise, he finds himself hired as a linguistic consultant for an intergalactic mission.

Exercise 4

What uses of, or beliefs about, or misapplications of magic most annoy and frustrate your magic user? And how does your character express that frustration? The tumblr thread I shared (above) is about getting a character to provide exposition *about* magic in a humorous or entertaining way, but a lecture may not be the only or first reaction your mage has to a misuse of or misconception about magic. Maybe your character will go out of their way to intervene. Or stand next to the offending person taking notes, only to deliver a sassy or cutting remark when the offender, infuriated at being observed and apparently documented, asks them what exactly they think they're doing. Maybe your mage just quietly undoes whatever the other person just did. Or they could show some other reaction. Write a brief dialogue or a scene that explores how your character reacts when another person does something with magic or says something about magic that seems innocuous (at first) to the reader but that infuriates or disturbs your character.

3. WHAT DO MAGES BELIEVE ABOUT THEIR MAGIC?

Before we close this chapter and leap into the actual design of your magic system, let's go one level deeper. Consider what your mages *believe* about their magic, about its nature, its origin, and its purpose.

What is the ultimate *reason* for magic in your created world? What does it *mean* to your characters? For Harry Dresden, Chicago's only professional wizard in Jim Butcher's novel *Storm Front*, magic is the primordial act of creation, of bringing things into existence. It is a fundamentally creative force. (Believing this, Dresden is sickened by uses of magic to destroy rather than create.) In C.S. Lewis's *The Lion, The Witch, and The Wardrobe,* magic alters the natural world through sacrifice, but the novel contrasts two ways of understanding sacrificial magic. The White Witch can cast spells of eternal winter and transform living beings into silent rock, sacrificing the lives of *others* in order to recreate the world for her pleasure. Aslan, on the other hand, thaws the ice and the stone. He resurrects himself and others by first giving himself to death on others' behalf. The Witch knows the Deep Magic from the Dawn of Time, but Aslan knows the Deeper Magic from Before the Dawn of Time.

Exercise 5

What is the "deeper magic" in *your* created world? In other words, *why does magic matter to your characters?* What do your characters believe magic is *for*? To explore how meaningful this question can be for a writer and to get creative with how the answers to it might play out, consider these two additional scenarios—two possibilities for what mages in a fictional story might believe about their magic:

1. *Magic is a gift.* In this case, your character believes magic to have been, originally, an act of hospitality. Perhaps your mage uses magic to multiply food for a guest at their table, or visits an old man with cataracts and gives light back to his eyes. Take a moment and jot down the following. For such a scenario, where magic's fundamental meaning is that it is a *gift*:

   What legend or bit of folklore does the mage in this world cherish, which expresses or explains how magic came into the world as a gift? How does that story shape the way they try to use magic?

   What do the people of this world consider to be a gift? Is a name a gift? Is a kiss a gift? Is a moment of silence a gift?

   What is the ultimate gift this mage could offer and might offer in the course of a short story or a novel? The gift that would cost the most to give, but that they must give if they're to be true to themselves, because that is what mages *do*?

   In what ways do other characters misuse magic to *take* rather than *give*? Does this cause your imagined protagonist rage, or grief, or horror?

   Imagine a scene in which the protagonist—who sees magic as a gift—uses it to take. What drives them to this choice? How do they feel about themselves after? Perhaps your mage invites an enemy to their home and violates their guest-right, using magic to cast them into an enchanted sleep and to take something from them while they slumber. Is this a 'necessary' choice that the mage perceives as being for the greater good, but one that costs them their self-respect and self-love? Or is it a moment when your mage gives in to the darkness?

2. *Magic is appetite.* In this case, your character believes that magic is a powerful, unstoppable expression of instinct, of hunger, of sexual lust, of fear, of our animal nature. It comes from the gut, from the loins, and from the belly, and not from the head. In this scenario:

What *happens* when someone casts a spell? Do they lose, for a time, their words and their intellect? Do they howl like a wolf, chatter like a bird? Does a woman grieving for the barrenness of a wilderness cast a spell to make a garden grow, and does she sway and creak like a tree, her hands moving like branches, during the spell?

What legend do the mages of *this* world tell about how magic came into their world?

How do lovers in this world use magic? How does a predator in this world use magic? What is the most intriguing character you can think of who might be a mage in this fictional world, where magic is *appetite*?

As you ponder what magic means to your characters, don't neglect to consider more personal feelings toward magic that your characters might have, feelings that aren't tied to cultural beliefs but instead to personal ambitions, dreams, and losses your characters have sustained. Sally Owens in Alice Hoffman's *Practical Magic* runs away from magic not because of anything she or others believe about what magic *is*, but because of what she personally feels that magic can't give her. Early in the novel, Sally grieves the death of a man she loved, realizing that magic can't bring him back. It is love and life—not just magic—that Sally is hiding from. What *personal* feelings do your characters have about magic, tied to their personal histories, to their greatest joys, to their hopes and fears, to their griefs?

My hope is that Exercise 5 has your creative juices flowing and has you ready to brainstorm and play. Because it's time to play, invent, and imagine. It's time to map the four elements of an unforgettable magic system: the costs, cultural function, mechanics, and ethics of magic.

2 | THE COSTS OF MAGIC

"MAGIC ALWAYS COMES AT A COST, DEARIE," Rumpelstiltskin glories in telling the heroines of *Once Upon a Time*. Most discussions of magic in classes on worldbuilding leave it at that. We'll have a lot more to cover in *this* book; nevertheless, we'll start with that idea of cost and devote this chapter to it. The costs of magic are important to consider not only because these keep your magic workers from being overpowered and boring, while simultaneously exerting pressures on your plot, but also because the specific costs, consequences, and risks of magic in your imagined world may prove to be intimately connected to and evocative of what kind of world you have made and what kind of story you are telling. And that's an exciting thing.

Because magic has a cost, using it means taking risks. Because magic users take risks, they have to make high-stakes choices under pressure. And *choices* are where your story happens. In this chapter, we'll look at examples of environmental, personal, and social costs—each of which is exciting in its own way. Toward the chapter's end, we'll also consider what opportunities for story might occur if costs are variable depending on the *source* of one's magic.

ENVIRONMENTAL COSTS

Today, the processes of industrial manufacturing exert considerable pressures on our own physical world; in an adjacent, fictional world, what pressures might *magic* exert? For example, if a mage multiplies the availability of a resource, are they subtracting it from somewhere else? If I magic a lake into existence in the midst of a desert, do several oases elsewhere dry up? In Margaret Weis and Tracy Hickman's *Fire Sea*, necromancers who raise the dead do so, without realizing it, by stealing life from other members of their species. When the Sartan necromancers undertake to raise *all* the dead, their species dwindles and faces extinction. And the witch Mirri Maz Duur at the end of George R. R. Martin's novel *A Game of Thrones* gives Daenerys a similarly dire warning: "Only life can pay for life."

Or, if summoning matter into existence in one place doesn't subtract it from somewhere else, does magic instead cause the physical world to warp and revolt, as though the universe panics or sickens at the mage's defiance of the laws of physics? In Richard Knaak's *Dragonrealm* novels, the most powerful wild magic distorts the physical world and ultimately wrecks it, bringing about desert wastelands and green, sickly skies of eternal tempest; after exhausting their planet, the mages of the Vraad flee their realm to seek another, bringing with them the wizardry and spellcraft that might spell the doom of their new world, too. Does magic used unwisely cause ecological or metaphysical crises in *your* invented world?

Is magic tied to a finite natural resource that can be spent or expended, like "Dust" in the world of the animated series *RWBY* or like the magic that the sorcerers of Qarth and the priestesses of Asshai use in George R. R. Martin's *A Song of Ice and Fire*? The magic of Qarth and Asshai is tied to dragons. When the dragons are gone from the world, magic fades; spells and rituals no longer do anything, like prayers to a god that has died. When dragons return, the magic comes back.

There may be environmental *constraints* as well as environmental *costs*. In *The Book of the New Sun* by Gene Wolfe, some herbs have to be drawn from grave soil by moonlight, or their magical properties are lost. In Thomas Malory's *Le Morte d'Arthur*, Sir Gawain drinks a potion and gains the strength to conquer a foe in battle, but only while the sun is high; as the day wanes, so does he—an echo of an older story of the sun deity on whose tales the earliest Gawain was based. Dracula can sleep only in his native soil, which must be carted in a coffin from Romania to England. Ghosts and the undead in Garth Nix's *Sabriel* (and in many other tales) cannot cross running water. In *The Dresden Files*, spells cast by night (except those cast by the strongest wizards) fade at daybreak.

Both costs and constraints create urgency in your story. A *cost* creates opportunities for tough choices. There may be consequences for casting a spell, consorting with a demon, making a garden grow wild with corn, or stepping nimbly from one world into another. A character may have to choose whether to raise their lover from the dead and face the dark costs of that act, or grieve and find closure. Or a witch might find it very tempting to raise someone from the dead after a lethal accident. Such choices aren't easy; for characters like Gillian and Sally Owens in *Practical Magic*, a forbidden act of resurrection may feel worth the cost…in the moment.

Similarly, a *constraint* creates urgency because it narrows the window in which your character might act, or imposes conditions that must be satisfied before the character can do what they wish. The simplest of all constraints is, of course, the *recipe*. Sometimes, very specific items might be needed for a spell, and these items may be hard to get. In the first issue of Neil Gaiman's comic *The Sandman,* Roderick Burgess wants to summon and imprison the Angel of Death. The recipe for that spell is a bit daunting:

> I give you a coin I made from a stone. I give you a song I stole from the dirt. I give you a knife from under the hills. And a stick that I stuck through a dead man's eye. I give you a claw I ripped from a rat. I give you a name, and the name is lost. I give you the blood from out of my vein, and a feather I pulled from an angel's wing.

> NEIL GAIMAN, *THE SANDMAN*

Imagine if your character had to collect those items! How might they do it? What might it cost them to pull a feather from an angel's wing?

Exercise 6

Knowing what you know *so far* about the magic you want to integrate into your story, into your fictional world or game, write down all the possible environmental costs of magic that you can imagine. Then, for each, write down options for how that cost might be mitigated (or paid).

If, for example, the use of magic drains all the light from a location for a day and a night, what do the villagers do while the mage is working their craft? If the village hires a mage to cast magic during the time of planting to ensure a bountiful harvest, do the villagers light a big bonfire (which nevertheless sheds only a pale light) and hold a celebration in defiance of darkness and winter, or do they all sit silently with hoods on, meditating on the dark and silent life of seeds under the earth, yearning for the sprouting to come?

Or, if the use of growing magic costs one year of someone's life, who pays that year? Does the village hold a lottery to determine whose life will be shortened by a year? Do they go kidnap someone from a neighboring village, for that purpose? Is there someone who, ceremonially, must fill that role—and does that person dread it, or do they feel honored? What if they choose to run away instead? Are they hunted through the last cold winter night before planting? Where do they find shelter? In a cave? In some cottage in the forest? Can they trust the old woman who lives there and offers them shelter?

Ah—now we have the beginning of a story! Maybe an exciting one.

Now take a look at your list of possible environmental costs and ways to mitigate or pay each cost. Which of these that you wrote down strikes you as especially compelling? Which one might conceal just inside it the seed, the kernel of a remarkable story or subplot?

Now do the same—this time with *constraints*. List possible constraints for some work of magic that you imagine could take place in your story. Then brainstorm what the mage might need to do, to satisfy those constraints. (What might it cost them to pull the feather from an angel's wing?)

Do you see any environmental costs or constraints that you may wish to include in your magic system? If so, take note of them and keep thinking about the exciting scenarios that may be possible with that particular cost and mitigation/payment strategy, or with that particular constraint.

PERSONAL COSTS
(TO MIND, BODY, OR SPIRIT)

By personal costs, I mean *costs to one's person*. In T.L. Morganfield's *The Bone Flower Throne*, the Aztec princess Quetzalpetlatl can work remarkable magic to protect her people—but she must sacrifice something of herself each time. To save her people from attack, to keep their blood from being shed, she cuts away some of her fingers on an altar, shedding blood of her own.

Personal costs of magic are exciting to imagine and write about, because a personal cost—a risk to the mind, body, or spirit—requires our characters to make riveting, high-stakes choices each time they wield magic. Perhaps your character can reshape the entire world, or make

STANT LITORE

armies of ghosts march on their foes, or feed an empire with a wave of her hand, but what will it cost her?

Raistlin in Margaret Weis and Tracy Hickman's *Dragonlance Chronicles* sacrifices his health; his body is weak, and he coughs up blood. But the toll on his *mind* is severe, too. He is a man of sharp intellect and cunning, but the cost he pays for his power is that his pupils are no longer circular but are shaped like hourglasses; everywhere he looks, he sees Time at work, sped up, unhidden. He sees his friends rot and decay, even as he sits down with them to eat a meal. Loneliness is his curse, and so he denies any need for fellowship. There is a daily, practical cost to each spell, too. Spells in Raistlin's world are very difficult to cast. They are primarily verbal, but each chant must be memorized, and the slightest error may prove lethal. Once the spell is cast, it is erased from the mage's mind, and if the mage wishes to cast it again, he must undertake the arduous work of relearning it, committing it to memory once more.

If artifacts in your world get imbued with magic, what impact do those artifacts have on the people who encounter them? Elric's blade Stormbringer in Michael Moorcock's novels is *hungry*; it must be fed. (Souls, specifically. The sword *needs* bloodshed.) The One Ring in J.R.R. Tolkien's *The Lord of the Rings* corrupts everyone who touches it, subsuming their identity until ultimately, if the Ring is with them long enough, they fade into a wraith or a puppet—unseen not only because of the magic of invisibility but because they no longer possess substance or reality.

Sebastian Balthazar Bux, in Michael Ende's *The Neverending Story*, can use the AURYN to grant his own wishes—but for each wish granted, he sacrifices one memory. After creating the world of Fantastica anew, filling it with wonders, he forgets who his friends are. He becomes selfish, cold, and callous—because he can't remember. In the end, he does not even remember his own name.

Exercise 7

Consider the following two scenarios:

1. *The use of magic has a heat expenditure.* When you run fast or exercise, your body heats up. The same happens when you cast a spell, and the heat expenditure of that magical effort is significant. Knowing this, what risks does a mage run? Do they need to take care not to wield magic in a hayloft or at a library or beside a gasoline pump, so as not to light it on fire? Does a mage who works extremely powerful magic run the risk of bursting into flames? Do mages soak themselves in ice water immediately before or after their magic? Do they wield magic naked, "skyclad," for relief from the heat? Do mages wear uniforms that are uniquely designed to shed the body's heat? On a cold winter night when the electrical power is out in the city, does your modern-day witch cast a spell making the forks and spoons dance cheerfully on the kitchen counter, just so the sudden burst of heat will warm the room? Think of the fun you could have with this!

2. *The use of magic is like a cash advance; it has to be repaid later.* So if you use magic to enhance your good luck, then you get especially bad luck later. Or if you use

magic to enhance the beauty of your appearance, then at the same time, unseen, your health declines…

For each of these scenarios, write a few paragraphs in which an elderly or ancient mage tells their apprentice the story of their most costly choice, sharing the tale of that spell and its consequences.

Exercise 8

Make a list of possible personal costs for magic. Which of these strike you as the most compelling or entertaining to write about? Which might you include in your own magic system?

SOCIAL COSTS

There have been times in our own world when people who were believed to be wielders of the arcane arts were shunned and avoided, or imprisoned, or burned, or drowned as witches. (And indeed, there are present-day countries where, at this very moment, people accused of witchcraft, even children, are tortured and disfigured.) Your fictional world may be such that the use of magic entails not simply a psychological, physical, or ecological cost, but also a social cost. Tara Abernathy, at the beginning of Max Gladstone's novel *Three Parts Dead*, wants to protect her remote, small town. She begins raising the dead and enchanting them as undead guardians, weaving shadow and grave rot about herself as she works her Craft. Coming suddenly upon her beside an open grave in the middle of the night and seeing a visible creature of darkness rather than a young woman of their own people, the villagers are ready to attack her. What might magic cost your characters in their relationships with others?

ISOLATION BECAUSE OTHERS FEAR THE MAGE

The primary social cost is usually *isolation*, and fear of the mage is certainly one thing that can cause that. The townspeople in a planet ravaged by wars of magic between the gods, in Max Gladstone's *Three Parts Dead*, fear those who wield magic, those who created the gods. A similar apprehension appears in the Netflix series *Arcane*; Professor Heimerdinger, over three centuries old, has founded the city of Piltover as a refuge from the violence of mages, which in the past has burned entire kingdoms out of existence. He is not quick to welcome the return of magic.

SELF-ISOLATION BECAUSE OF DANGER TO OTHERS

That phobia of others toward a mage is a social cost that surfaces frequently in fiction. But it isn't the only one. Kahlan in Terry Goodkind's series *The Sword of Truth* is lonely not because she is feared but because she must remain celibate, even if falling in love; to lose herself in ecstasy would risk "confessing" her lover, drawing out their soul and transforming them into a will-less slave. And DC's comic book character John Constantine lives an isolated life both because each day, he sees horrors that would drive other people mad and because the people he gets close to have a tendency to die horribly. For characters like Kahlan and Constantine, it is not others' fear of them that is the issue but their own fear of consequences to others that their lives as magic users may entail.

ISOLATION BECAUSE OF THE HORRORS THE MAGE HAS SEEN

Seeing the horrors that others remain unaware of, or perceiving and experiencing reality in a fundamentally different way than others perceive and experience it, can prove isolating in and of itself. Raistlin in *Dragonlance* isn't lonely because others fear him; he is lonely because he sees everyone aging, decrepit and dying before his eyes. Bran Stark, in the televised adaptation of *Game of Thrones* Seasons 7-8, gains the ability to see past and future but loses much of his hold on the present, becoming distant, appearing nearly emotionless, barely present around those who love him. As in Plato's allegory of the cave, the one who has seen and cannot forget a reality that remains hidden from others finds themselves an exile among those who haven't seen what *they* have seen.

THE BURDEN OF RESPONSIBILITY

Similarly, the burden of responsibility can isolate a magic user. In my own novel *What Our Eyes Have Witnessed*, Father Polycarp bears the burden of witness. He serves a function similar to the folkloric "sin eater"; when the hungry dead threaten to devour the living, Polycarp can grasp one of the ghouls by its shoulder or its arm, gaze into its eyes, and see everything that person had been when they were alive. Everything they ever feared and felt, every grief and every regret, every joy and every hope, every lost love. He can see them "as nakedly as God does," with no veil between his soul and theirs. In that moment, he can absolve them of all their pain and grant them rest. The soul comes back into the eyes of the hungry corpse and finds peace at last; the zombie slumps down, lifeless, onto the stones of the street. But there is an intense psychological and social cost to seeing others' souls so nakedly, so completely. Witnessing all these lives makes Polycarp sorrowful and it makes him kind, but it also makes him very lonely.

THE CASSANDRA EFFECT

The Cassandra Effect or Cassandra Curse is another way that the burden of responsibility or the burden of witness can isolate someone who has touched another world or been visited by the supernatural. Cassandra of Troy is granted the gift of prophecy, but having spurned a god, she is also doomed with the curse that no one will ever believe her. She can forsee the fall of her city, the brutal deaths of her loved ones, her rape by a Greek soldier, all of it before it occurs, but no one believes her. She is mocked and despised for her gift. Yet it is not the mockery that is her burden but the *grief* of seeing what will happen while being able to do nothing about it.

Suffering the Cassandra Effect a little differently, Samuel Taylor Coleridge's old wayfarer in *The Rime of the Ancient Mariner* witnesses the deaths of everyone else on his ship, and their undeaths as well, as they rise, moaning, from the deck to climb the rigging and unfurl the sails once more. He sees mermaids dance on the waves and many things besides, and for the rest of his life, he tries to tell others what he has seen. He becomes frantic with the need to share the experience with someone, anyone, to be *not alone*. But the strangers he approaches think him a drunkard, a madman, or a nuisance, and flee his approach. While not a mage per se, the Ancient Mariner provides an additional example of the costs your spellcaster could face. Perhaps you have a character who walks through others' dreams or who unexpectedly finds themselves planeswalking through realms of horror, skipping across a thousand hells like a pebble across a lake. When they make it back again to the waking world or to the world of the living, if they try to tell what they have seen, how might they be despised or disbelieved!

Exercise 9

Make a list of possible social costs for magic. Which of these strike you as the most compelling or entertaining to write about? Which social costs—for your particular character—would invoke most cruelly their own fears and personal wounds? Which costs might require the most fortitude, courage, or endurance? Which social costs might they find it least easy to bear? After all, the exciting thing about coming up with a cost for magic is discovering for yourself how your mage will bear that cost, what choices they will make in doing so, and what kind of person they may become. The cost of magic makes Raistlin remorseless, Polycarp kind, the Ancient Mariner desperate. What choices will your character make when they have to pay the price of their magic? Who will they discover themselves to be? What sort of person will they become? Write down the possibilities that occur to you, and then consider: Which social costs might you include in your own magic system?

VARIABLE COSTS
DEPENDING ON THE *SOURCE*
OF YOUR MAGIC

One more wrinkle to consider is the question of source. In Robert Jordan's *The Wheel of Time*, the Source of magic has two sides, a masculine half and a feminine half, but in his fictional world, the masculine half has been tainted, and to draw power from that half of the Source sickens and maddens the mind. Male mages go mad, violently so, and to prevent this, young men capable of wielding magic are hunted down and "gentled" (severed from the Source, magically castrated) by female mages. Though the gender politics of Jordan's worldbuilding are fraught, the example of his Aes Sedai raises an intriguing question for writers: What is your mage's relationship to the *source* of their magic? You can get very playful and inventive in answering this.

For example, suppose you have a world in which mages channel the power or the favor of gods. (Perhaps your mages are actually clerics, and all magic is a form of prayer.) If so, do different gods grant magic differently, entailing different costs? Maybe a god of mischief will win the lottery for you, but you need to perform a spectacularly good prank on someone in order to merit the trickster's favor. Maybe the god who brings both disease and healing will cure your ailing sister, but only if you first care for a sick bird, taking in the little skysinger and nursing it back to health, or only if you fund an apothecary, or only if you take the illness into yourself instead. If there is 'good' magic and 'evil' magic in your story, are these named so because of their effects, or because of their source?

You might also think about magical devices that incur different costs, such as, again, the One Ring in J.R.R. Tolkien's *The Lord of the Rings*, which can make you invisible or give you power over what others see and feel, over their perspective and their will—but at the terrible cost of sacrificing your own will, your own identity and corporeal reality, fading with time.

Exercise 10

Consider this scenario. Perhaps the source of magic is the moon, and it can be tapped into by drinking still water that reflects the moonlight. As you drink the light, the power of the moon fills you, and you can perform wondrous and unexpected feats. But do you get different effects and different costs if you are drinking the clearest water from a mountain pool versus, in desperation, the water shimmering on the side of the street, dirty and tainted? Do you get different effects depending on whether the moon is full, quarter, or crescent-sliver? In a world with multiple moons, like Krynn in Margaret Weis and Tracy Hickman's

Dragonlance novels, perhaps it matters *which* moon you are tapping into. And what does the moonlight do in your body, once you've drunk it? Does it make you tipsy, rendering it more difficult to focus on the spell you need to cast? Does it make you begin your next menstrual cycle early (in fact, that very night), so that the casting of magic entails personal discomfort and cramping? Does it cast you into a dream-state, or awaken wild appetites? Does it bring you dreams once you sleep, prophetic dreams that might be soothing or disturbing, depending on their content (or perhaps depending on the lunar phase)? What costs might your moon cleric incur when drinking moonlight? Write a few paragraphs exploring this.

Exercise 11

Write down all the sources of magic you can think of that could possibly be included in your fiction. Does all magic come from the same place? Or from varied sources? Is magic looked upon differently depending on its source? What costs does each source entail? Which of these options that you can imagine is most compelling to you? Which might you include in the magic system in your story?

3 | THE CULTURAL FUNCTION OF MAGIC

NOW IMAGINE A FICTIONAL COMMUNITY in which witches are sought after as urgently and pragmatically as plumbers or firefighters are. In this imagined world, witches are called "swifts." Most other people, everyday people, "sing their spells" to enchant the world (so to speak) by means of the actions they take and the choices they make, but they exert their influence only slowly, in an everyday way. It takes four decades of arduous work to mold part of the world to your will. But a witch, a "swift," is a *swiftsinger*, enchanting the world and enacting her will quickly, in the course of mere hours or even minutes. Need to replant a forest after clear cutting? Call in a swift to press her palms to the soil and sing. Need a wound to seal itself up and heal? Call in a swift who can sing to flesh and bone.

What we name things matters, because names are a kind of storytelling, and are a method by which we shape and transmit our culture. By looking at what we call a particular profession or vocation, we can learn quite a bit about its cultural function and impact, which is to say, what that vocation *means* to people—both those within it and those outside it.

Consider the various words for *magic user* with which we are already most familiar. Both *wizard* and *witch* derive etymologically from the word for *wise*; a wizard or a witch is one who knows secret lore and understands the world in which they live more deeply than others do. The word *enchanter* is derived from a verb meaning *to sing*, and it is related to our words *chant, canto, incantation, canticle*, and even *Chanticleer* (the rooster whose crowing song wakes the sun and brings our day star back into the sky each morning); an enchanter is one who sings things into reality, wooing possibilities across the boundary from the imagined to the real by the power of their voice. *Sorcerer* and *sorceress* come from Latin *sors*, which meant the answer an oracle gives you about the future, and that in turn is derived (we think) from a Proto-Indo-European verb that meant "to bind"; a sorcerer binds spirits and bids them speak, to get information about the unseen world or information about the visible world that is nonetheless concealed, or information about what has not yet come to be. The term *warlock* (often used of a worker of "black magic" or of a magus with malevolent ends or with malevolent means of reaching his ends) comes from Old English *wærloga*, meaning a deceiver or one who has been faithless (literally, a breaker of truces). What a distance there is, between the words *wizard* and *warlock*! Think about how different some of these terms actually are, and what each implies about the culture that gave that name to a magic user. (Of course, various people in your story, even within one culture, may feel differently about magic users, and may even use different words to refer to them. Exploring why these differences exist and why some of them run deep can be useful.)

Exercise 12

We opened this chapter imagining a community that calls its magic users *swifts*. What does your fictional community call its mages? Come up with a new word for a magic user, one that we have never heard before. Within your fiction, what does this new word mean? Where does the word come from? Does everyone *understand* the word in the same way? (For example, in contemporary American culture, witches may understand the word *witch* to be derived from *wise one*, but others may associate derogatory connotations with the word.) Do your characters who are magic users adopt the word or label with pride? Is it a word that was weaponized against them but that they have now reclaimed and repurposed as their own? Do multiple terms for magic user exist, and how might these different terms capture and illustrate different characters' attitudes toward magic and its uses? What do these words imply about the function that magic users perform within their community?

Exercise 13

Write a page exploring, from your mage's perspective, what magic workers are, what they do, and what that means to your character. This needn't be pure exposition; instead, have your magic user speak what is in their heart to another person, telling what they are and why. To *really* explore what magic means, culturally, in your story, do this exercise several times:

- Have your character explain and define themselves to a hostile listener.
- Have your character explain and define themselves to their child.
- Have your character explain and define themselves on a first date.
- Have your character explain and define themselves when asked by the most respected and revered magic user in their world.

Each of these variations will bring out different emotions and different intensities on the part of your character. Each will require them to make a case (whether implicitly or explicitly) for why magic and magic workers are important to their culture, or for why they should act as they do. In the same way that a kindergarten teacher might explain what a teacher is (and why *they* are one) with differing emphasis and intensity depending on whether they are defending education at a congressional hearing, telling their child what kind of work they do, or speaking to a blind date about their work, in analogous scenes your mage will also reveal different things about who and what they are, how they feel about that, and how they expect others to respond to them. And perhaps one of the scenes in this exercise will ignite such a passion and a fire in your mage that you will find them speaking lines that become thematically significant and critical to your story.

HOW DO PEOPLE FEEL
ABOUT MAGIC USERS?

As you consider what your mages are *called*, consider both how other see them and what role mages assume within your fictional community. Are mages common? Are they revered or hated? If a mage can teleport around the world, is the cost they experience that they see the world in a fundamentally different way from everyone else? For a person who wields no magic and must rely on their feet to get about, another country may be an inconceivably distant place, perhaps strange and to be feared. For the mage, another country may be just another room in the house, taking only a moment to step into or out of. Are mages the *de facto* diplomats of such a world? Or, consider how differently your mage might perceive not only physical distance but also the necessity of social niceties and the complex dynamics between hosts and guests. Maybe your mage treats such things frivolously; being able to pop into and out of any city or house at will, maybe they see little point in knocking at a door. Or maybe they treat such things more seriously than everyone else does; maybe your mage, like a vampire, will never enter any place uninvited. Indeed, maybe they *can't*; maybe people put up magical wards just as they put up physical locks on their homes, or maybe—as in Jim Butcher's *The Dresden Files*—thresholds crossed without permission tend to break and weaken the visitor's magic.

WRITE MAGIC SYSTEMS YOUR READERS WON'T FORGET

When you are either uncertain where to start or when you want to go back and check if your understanding of the cultural implications of your magic system are now written deep into the bones of your story, here is a quick and easy way to start gathering clues as to what magic might mean, culturally, in your fictional world. Answer the question: *What feelings does it evoke in non-magic-users in your story, when they witness magic?*

For example, does magic evoke *wonder*? In Studio Ghibli's anime film *Kiki's Delivery Service*, townspeople gaze up with wonder and sudden delight when young Kiki flits between buildings on her broom. Does magic evoke *horror*, as in the fiction of Robert E. Howard, where Conan might prefer a good arm wrestling contest over having to deal with a sorcerer who can turn himself into a snake? Does magic evoke the *numinous*, a sense that the character witnessing the magic is seeing something both otherworldly and holy? Does it evoke *hope* in human capacity and progress? In the steampunk world of Netflix's series *Arcane*, seeing master technicians harness magic convinces some in the city of Piltover that their faith in the inevitability and benevolence of "progress" will be rewarded, and that their people will be able to overcome any obstacle and heal any sickness; some see dollar signs; others respond with *fear*, remembering ancient times when mages obliterated entire civilizations with magic.

To discover what magic means to a culture, explore what people feel in response to it, and why, and where those feelings come from.

Exercise 14

Return to the spell or magical incident that you described in Exercise 1. Now describe that magical incident from different perspectives:

- Your mage's child (or sibling or other family member) witnesses the spell or magical incident. How do they feel, witnessing it?
- Your mage's love interest sees it. How do they feel about it?
- The mayor or leader of the community sees it. How do they feel about it?
- Someone living on the street—someone in poverty, or perhaps an outcast from the community—witnesses it. How do they feel about it?
- A more prominent and skilled magic user witnesses it. How do they feel about it?

In each case, you want to use this exercise to explore how each character feels about magic, what their culture tells them about magic, and whether their feelings and beliefs are in accord with or in defiance of what their culture teaches about magic.

Exercise 15

Create a myth or legend about how magic came to *be*. Prometheus stole fire from the gods to give it to humanity; Adam's theft of a fruit condemned humanity to agriculture in a broken world, to having to toil and sweat and bleed in order to coax an unkind earth into producing food. Who stole *magic*? Who brought magic into your fictional world, and how did they do it, and why? When mothers tell their children that tale, what moral do they attach to the end of it?

Exercise 16

Imagine a fictional community in which magic has been *absent,* though remembered. Create a legend or folktale about what it will be like when magic comes back. For example, slaves in Louisiana and the Caribbean used to tell stories that one day, an old man would visit their hovels and teach them magic, and then they would grow wings and fly back to Africa. With this story of magic came the hope of freedom, an end to exile, and power over their own lives. For your fictional community where magic is felt or believed to be absent, what do people feel when they dream of its return? Do they imagine the restoration of a golden past? Or a storm that will destroy their present prosperity? Will magic come upon them one day, swift and destructive, like locusts in the crops? Or will it come to them as a miracle, so that the blind will see and the lame will leap and walk? Jot down a summary of the story such characters might tell anticipating magic's return. Perhaps you will discover a specific meaning and significance to magic that you can import into the story you're writing.

WHAT ROLE DO MAGIC USERS HAVE IN THE COMMUNITY?

In Slavic folklore, if you are a young person (particularly a young woman) wandering in the woods, you might encounter an old woman with long nails and piercing eyes who lives in a hut that strides about on the legs of a chicken. Baba Yaga's magic is as wild as the deepest, darkest part of the forest. One cannot ever be quite sure what will happen or what she will do. She might eat you. She might set you three impossible tasks or tests. She might (if you earn it) present you with a magical artifact that will return with you to your village. She is perilous and deadly, but she is not the old witch in the gingerbread house who wishes to fatten and devour poor Hansel and Gretel; it is not *hunger* the lost child sees in her eyes, but *cunning*. Wild as she is, Yaga has a role to play, one that can only be played from her position outside of the community, in the wild night. She prepares the young Slav for adulthood and for their responsibilities, because her tests (and indeed, the ultimate test of surviving an encounter with her) force the youth to grow in ways they could not have imagined growing while comfortably at home. To survive and even thrive in a winter world, the young person must become hard, cunning, and enduring as water beneath the ice, but nevertheless without losing their compassion for others. To encounter Baba Yaga is to learn what you are made of, and to be tempered like steel before returning to your village.

Yaga has a specific role—to *test and temper* the young— but she is also more than just her role, even as real people are more than theirs. She has her own sense of wild humor, her cackling glee at riding on the wind in a flying mortar and pestle, her primeval hungers, and her rages if she is tricked.

Conversely, the Yoruba magic worker who lives in a West African or Caribbean community works in the midst of their people, offering insight from the spiritual world to any who need it and are willing to take the necessary risk of hearing it. For the Yoruba, each child forgets their destiny in the shock of being born, with that first birthcry; the task of a human being is to rediscover their destiny— and live it. To do this, a type of magic or insight is needed; because we do not know our own destinies, we must consult those who do, either spirits of the world unseen or our ancestral dead, who know our destiny because before we were born we sat with them discussing it. The seer in the village doesn't *test* or *temper* the young, as Baba Yaga does; instead, their role is to help the young hear themselves more clearly and see their purpose more plainly.

The *role* (or, as I called it in the title of this chapter, the "cultural function") of the mage can help shape their position in the community, as well as the type of magic they wield (and when, and for whose benefit), and even the type of home they live in and the type of costume and accoutrements they wear. Either Baba Yaga or the Yoruba seer might tell a young person a bit of their future, but they do so for different purposes, and one would never expect to find them wearing the same garb or living in the same type of house. And, of course, young people feel very differently depending on which of these characters they are consulting.

It is useful to consider how mages are separate from their community *and* how they are integral to, or integrated into, it (to the extent that they are). Do you call a magic user when a certain problem arises, the way you call a doctor when you have an injury or the Ghostbusters when you have a haunted attic? What problems might mages respond to? Or, do mages live in hiding? (Do people still seek them out?) Do non-magical characters visit the local conjure woman or fortune teller for advice? If this is frowned upon, what might drive someone to do so anyway? (Answering that, you suddenly have the kernel or seed for a story...)

Exercise 17

Write a *job ad* for a magic user. What are they being hired for? What qualifications and experience do they need to demonstrate? What will they be paid? Is it a salaried position, or commission? And what got the mage they're replacing fired?

Exercise 18

Write a *resume* for a magic user. Where did they go to school? (Or, who did they apprentice under?) What jobs have they had in the past that required the use of their magic? (You can have a lot of fun with this; maybe your mage is being hired to as an exorcist, and they list their first job as a sewer maintenance engineer, which actually means that they spent weary nights sludging though the sewers of New York catching ghost alligators.) Who do they put down as references?

Exercise 19

Write a *letter of reference* for a magic user who is applying for a job, for graduate school, for apprenticeship to a powerful mage, or to something else that tickles your imagination. What does their old mentor have to say about them? What incidents do they describe to paint the portrait of this young mage that they have such hopes for? What flaws do they try to contextualize or sugarcoat? "Yes, Archimedes *is* a bit too earnest at times, and did once miscast a spell resulting in half the population of Argos being replaced by grandfather clocks striding about on wooden legs, *but* that very eagerness is what has driven him to achieve the highest grades and pursue uses of transmutation that even our best and wisest here had scarcely begun to imagine. He will be a credit to your society, and I earnestly request that you enroll him in your member list and welcome him into your august body, grandfather clocks and all."

Remember, too, that one person's microwave might be another person's witchcraft. Arthur C. Clarke coined the law that "any sufficiently advanced technology is indistinguishable from magic," and consequently, you can imagine scenarios in which mages truly *are* scientists, technicians, artists, and engineers whose work is simply incomprehensible to others. Even in *The Lord of the Rings*, the Elves are repeatedly confused when the hobbits refer to their healing craft and their use of devices for seeing the future as "magic." To them, it's lore; it's knowledge. Several times, the Elves profess to not quite understand what the hobbits mean by "magic." There might be similar divisions at play in your own story.

THE QUESTION OF COVENS

Throughout this chapter, I've been saying *mage* and *magic worker* as if a magical act is something performed by a single person.

STANT LITORE

Is it?

As you think about how the culture in your story (whether the culture of a village, a city, a civilization, or simply the subculture of a big multigenerational family) responds to and defines magic, think too about whether magic is an individual or communal experience, or both at different times and for different purposes. Some spells might require a community to cast them. In Toni Morrison's *Beloved*, an angry ghost can only be exorcised by an entire community united in song. In Robert Jordan's fantasy series *The Wheel of Time*, it takes a circle of thirteen Aes Sedai in order to sever someone from the Source of magic, and the creation and use of some magical artifacts requires the cooperation of male and female mages. The reasons for needing a coven, a team, or a squadron of battle mages could be practical ones. Magic is an attempt to enact one's will upon the world, but the world may be resistant to change, and it may require multiple spellcasters to coax the world to do as the mages wish. Or there may be an ethical reason for needing a coven, a crew, or a council of mages rather than a single wizard, witch, or enchanter; perhaps some magic should only be done with the consent and participation of a community, since the outcome of that magic will affect them all.

An analogy can be drawn with the use of prayer in Eastern Orthodox Christianity (and with other forms of supplication in several other religious traditions). Just as a coven of mages may gather to *tell* the world to change in a certain way, a body of clerics and laity gather to *request* it. In the Greek Orthodox faith, it is believed that when the faithful chant a liturgical prayer that has also been chanted by many other gatherings of the faithful in the past, and that will be chanted again by many in the future, then all the faithful in all places and at all times are praying together; because God perceives all of time simultaneously, he hears all of those prayers as one prayer, sees his people as all asking together in one spirit and with one accord, and is moved to respond with love and compassion. Each person's prayer is intensely personal, and yet no prayer is solitary, because it is also being prayed by others among the faithful, including those who lived long ago and those who have yet to be born.

So, in your fiction, do your mages act as solitary figures, as lone wizards and wanderers like Gandalf the Grey, or do they require a fellowship, a gathering of the faithful, a council, a coven, or a committee? Is magic communal? Does it have a liturgy, a recitation, a call and a response, a ritual? Does it include religious activities and beliefs? These are all questions that can especially help you imagine the uses of magic if the culture in your fictional world is a communal one, or one less informed and less inspired by Western cultures than by other cultures around the world.

Or perhaps your fictional mages are reacting *against* a communal culture. Maybe everyone else approaches life communally, but the magic workers are forever separated from that communal experience. Or you may be writing a very individualistic culture, but the *mages* are communal, and the challenge each mage faces is to set aside their individual striving and unite with their group. In fact, you could even write a story where an individual's flailing about with magic to satisfy their own ego, pride, ambition, or desire is the *problem*. Or you could write a story where a community has become calcified, restrictive, and controlling, and the individual's magic becomes resistance and self-expression. Or you could write within a fictional world where neither of those possibilities accurately represents the whole story.

Perhaps the coven of witches is where the heroine of your tale discovers her allies, acknowledges her full power, and completes the heroine's journey. In *Practical Magic*, Sally Owens begins the novel as an outsider in her community but ends the novel united with the women of her community in a rite of exorcism, presenting a united front against an invading spirit, a male interloper invading women's bodies and women's spaces. Together, the women of the village exult in the rescue of Sally's sister, and together, they take up their brooms to sweep the ashes and grave dirt of the exorcised spirit out of the house. This communal act of magic transforms the community into one in which *all* the women participating are empowered, and in which Sally at last has an honored and integral place, where she can live and love freely and fully, and cast her own unique magic. (For more on the heroine's journey, distinct from the "hero's journey," see Gail Carriger's book *The Heroine's Journey*. It is an excellent resource, and every writer should have a copy.)

MAGIC AND MORTALITY

Does magic cheat death? Or does it make the fragility of life both more visible and meaningful? What is the relationship between *magic* and *mortality* in your fiction?

This can be a fruitful topic to think through. One of the reasons that culture exists is to provide comfort in the face of death, to give *life* and *death* meaning, to present us with narratives and rituals that articulate, perpetuate, and enforce that meaning. As a writer, you can have a lot of fun asking how the culture in your story provides comfort around mortality, and how magic factors into that. In your fictional culture, do people hide their elders away in assisted living campuses, or do the old and the dying live among their children? Are the old feared, honored, celebrated, humored, or respected? When children die young, how do the people in your story-world grieve? In medieval England, there was once a practice of burying dead infants under the eaves of a church, so that when it rained, the water would trickle down on the tiny graves; the "angels' tears," it was said, would bless the tiny souls who were gone, and they would be baptized in that rain and welcomed to paradise.

What does the culture in *your* story do?

And how is magic integrated into that, or disruptive to it?

Culture defines, explains, and protects boundaries (between past and present, between classes and castes of people, between genders, between childhood and adulthood, between single and joined in love or matrimony, between kin and stranger, between included and excluded, and between life and death). Magic bursts in, disrupts those boundaries, and turns things upside down. The eggshell broken over the frying pan drops out a live chick instead of a yolk; a sudden snow is summoned on Christmas morning out of a clear sky in Texas. A crystal ball or a *palantir* grants a glimpse of a possible future, transgressing the boundary we perceive between *today* and *tomorrow*. The boundary that we tend to regard as the most fixed in place is that between *life* and *death*. Does your magic system include possibilities for crossing that boundary, and if so, how does the culture you're writing feel about that?

Exercise 20

Make a list of boundaries that *could* get crossed within your magic system, and then note how the culture in your story describes those boundaries. Which boundaries are risky for a mage to cross for practical reasons (because the magic may backfire, or they may get lost in the icy waters of death themselves, or there may be some other significant cost to that crossing)? Which are risky for cultural reasons (crossing *this* boundary here gets a mage thanked, but crossing *that* boundary there gets them burned at the stake)? Take a good look at your list of boundaries that might be crossed or shattered. It's a recipe for storytelling opportunities!

Here are a few of my own favorite examples just to get you thinking: In Ursula K. Le Guin's *A Wizard of Earthsea*, Ged Sparrowhawk must cross into the country of death, calling the name of a child who is dying, asking them to turn back. Too late. That child crosses a threshold beyond which there is no return and beyond which Ged cannot follow. Later, Ged defeats a dragon that was terrifying the further islands, yet on one island he will always be unwelcome, because he is the wizard who can knock a dragon out of the sky but cannot save a feverish child. In Garth Nix's *Sabriel*, the titular character has the task of sending the unquiet and violent dead back where they belong, and her ability to cross the boundaries between life and death brings her both peril (from the dead) and honor and respect (from the living). In Margaret Weis and Tracy Hickman's *Fire Sea*, an underground civilization employs necromancers who raise the dead to serve as a compliant and unpaid labor force. Here, necromancers are an integral and accepted part of their society, but to the readers' horror, it is revealed that each act of resurrection results in the untimely death of another person. There is a steep cost to their magic—just not a *social* cost. In Robert E. Howard's *The Hour of the Dragon*, the act of raising an ancient sorcerer from the dead has unintended consequences when that sorcerer from ages past attempts to resurrect their entire past civilization, not just its people but its cities and its glory. The sorcerer Xaltotun sacrifices the living in secret rituals in the wilderness to revivify his long-dead world. At moments, the ancient world is superimposed over the present one, a shadow-image that, if it becomes real, will replace the world in which the characters of the story live, breathe, and act. As these stories each suggest, perhaps there is no magic more seductive than that used to speak to the dead, or to return them to the fields we know, or to turn back the relentless clock hands of time. As a writer committing your own wild magic on the page, you get to have the fun of discovering what such acts of resurrection cost your mages, how their communities perceive those acts and those who commit them, and what character-defining choices your mages will make during their brushes with the darker arts.

4 | THE MECHANICS OF MAGIC: HOW DOES IT WORK?

YOU'VE THOUGHT ABOUT THE *WHY* and the *what* of magic; now let's think about the *how*. Let's talk about spells and tools, devices and rituals—the mechanics or mechanisms of your magic system. If you think of magic as a *grammar* for your fictional world (a set of principles and practices which govern, empower, and constrain action within that world), a kind of language system by which magic users can understand their world and speak incredible effects into it—then think of spells and devices as the *vocabulary*, comprising the words, phrases, incantations, or ingredients that one must have ready if one is to speak power or healing into a magic-susceptible world.

SPELLS

No two vocabularies in our own world sound the same; German and French sound very different, as do Tsalagi, Finnish, and Swahili. Just as linguistic vocabularies are each distinct and unique (though not unrelated), the library of spells in your fictional world may also be distinct. The spellcraft you devise for your imagined society and its characters determines both the opportunities and limits of their magic and its flavor. So let's take a look at some of the choices you have for devising a magical vocabulary, at some (by no means all) of the options for how spells can *work*. As you review these examples and complete the exercises, new ideas beyond those hinted at in these pages may occur to you that could prove both unexpected and exciting. To get you thinking, we'll look at spellcraft that is based on *correspondences*, on *evocation* and *thaumaturgy*, on *songs and naming*, and on *playing the probabilities*. These four represent quite different (though not mutually exclusive) approaches to the mechanics of spellcasting.

CORRESPONDENCES

The simplest (yet perhaps most intricate) magical vocabularies are built on the basis of correspondences, whereby a mage integrates various items into their magic that each suggest or represent something symbolically. For example, consider the ingredients for a lust spell in Jim Butcher's novel *Storm Front*:

8 ounces of tequila (to lower inhibitions)

3 ounces of dark chocolate

A drop of perfume

An ounce of shredded lace

A sigh

Candlelight

Ashes of a passionate love letter (or, if such a letter proves unavailable, then the ashes of an erotic scene on pages torn from a romance novel)

Powder from a diamond or a torn up fifty-dollar bill (because "money is sexy")

The scene where this potion is mixed is played for humor; Harry Dresden had intended to brew a *love* potion (with a liquid base of champagne rather than tequila, for example), but he gives in and follows the instructions of his supernatural advisor Bob the Skull, despite his worry that Bob's recipe for this potion may produce "a sleazier result."

The potions in Dresden's magic system consist of eight ingredients: a liquid base, five ingredients to engage the senses, one for each (chocolate for *taste*, perfume for *smell*, lace for *touch*, a sigh for *sound*, and candlelight for *sight*), something to engage the spirit, and something to engage the mind. Each of the ingredients is selected based on a correspondence. Chocolate suggests or *corresponds* to pleasure and delight; lace suggests erotic intimacy; and a sigh suggests longing.

For the potions *your* mages will create, you might use more complex correspondences, too. For example, your magic system might require that a love or lust potion needs to be prepared beneath a full moon, the lovers' moon. Or perhaps your mage needs to face in a specific direction while mixing the potion. If, for example, in your fiction the four cardinal directions are each assigned their traditional Western European correspondences:

North	Earth	Body, material concerns
West	Water	Heart, emotion
South	Fire	Spirit, passion
East	Air	Mind, intellect

...then perhaps your mage needs to be facing *west* and standing in a moonlit pond while mixing their ingredients if they intend to make a love potion to work their will upon the heart, or else facing *south* and brewing the potion over a crackling fire if they intend a *lust* potion to work their will upon the passions. Dresden's magic in *Storm Front* is simpler than that; I mention these possibilities just to offer examples of the types of correspondences you can write into a magic system as you design the parameters for how spells in your story are supposed to work. A magic system, after all, can be as complex or as simple as you prefer, as complex or simple as the story needs it to be.

You can imagine all manner of correspondences—or research them, if your magic system is one that exists, culturally, in our own world, or is meant to suggest a historical magic system. For example, consider this set of Western European correspondences:

Moon	Sun
Feminine	Masculine
White	Yellow
Moonstone	Gold
Change	Stability
Wildness	Strength
Dreams, illusion	Waking, intellect
Doe	Lion
Alder	Oak
Milk	Mead

Let's suppose that, drawing upon such a symbolic vocabulary, your magical artisan creates an enchanted stained glass window. Depicted in the stained glass, a sated and satisfied lion lies sleeping in the embrace of three white does on a carpet of moonstones, on the bank of a river of milk, beneath an oak tree that is embraced by three intertwining alders, beneath a full moon. The stained glass appears above the altar in the temple to the moon goddess, and men who stand beneath that stained glass, their faces touched by its light, fall swiftly into waking dreams of love. Soon the sorcerous priestesses of the temple lead the men away to recessed alcoves, there to consummate their passion and their magic. An entire magical vocabulary is written into that stained glass and then activated by moonlight.

Exercise 21

> Conversely, what would a stained glass window in the temple of the sun god look like, and what would happen to those who stood bathed in *his* light? Either drawing upon the correspondences listed on the previous page or creating a list of your own correspondences for the *sun*, write several paragraphs describing that stained glass window in the sun temple, and what magic is worked upon those who turn their faces toward its light.

What if the culture in your story doesn't have these familiar correspondences, but instead quite different ones? For some Western cultures, the Moon was a woman (or a triad of women), and the Sun a man. But for the Norse, the Sun was female and the Moon was male. (That's why we have nursery rhymes and lore, even today, about "the man in the moon"; that's where he comes from.) For the ancient Egyptians, both Moon and Sun were male. Perhaps in *your* fictional culture, the Moon, changeable and lovely as it cycles through its phases, is instead nonbinary or shifts gender and appearance at will.

It is possible that reading about symbolic (or magical) correspondences in this chapter may fascinate you—or it may feel daunting. If the latter, just think of all the correspondences that we accept as obvious in our own contemporary culture. For example, if you are reading this book in the United States, you will probably recognize any and all of the following as symbolically suggestive of love and desire:

Hearts
Roses
Red/pink
X's and O's

These correspondences are written so pervasively into our culture's symbolic vocabulary that we don't even have to think about them or put any effort into deciphering them; if someone sends us a red rose or a heart-shaped box of chocolates, or signs their email with X's and O's, we know immediately what is being conveyed. Or think of how specific decorations and even specific colors are associated with particular American holidays. Look at the list below. Which holiday is this?

Pumpkins
Orange and black

Bats
Spiders
Broomsticks
Candy

Halloween—we recognize it immediately. Similarly, reds, browns, and earth tones, autumn leaves, a cornucopia, and a turkey mean *Thanksgiving* and *harvest*, while red, green, and white, milk and cookies, stockings, coniferous trees, reindeer, and Nativity scenes all immediately evoke *Christmas*. And so on. My point is that however mundane or non-magical our lives might appear to be, we are nonetheless relying on symbolic correspondences all the time. Your fictional mages may well do the same but will use these correspondences not only to wish for peace and goodwill toward men, but to make it so.

To a limited degree, many people who decorate their homes or vehicles, intentionally using correspondences, do entertain some faith that these decorations have a local impact on their world, if only to bring cheer or a spirit of gratitude into their neighborhood. And a pickup truck decked out with American flags, religious and political bumper stickers, and an image of a coiled-up rattlesnake with the inscription "Don't tread on me," and with a Confederate flag to boot, is *almost* intended to be an enchanted truck, on which a spell has been worked to invoke and bring about a certain version of America, though it would likely irritate the driver if we were to tell him he was practicing rudimentary witchcraft. More benignly, a non-mage will put a Christmas wreath on their door, and a mage will put an enchanted wreath on *her* door; the difference lies not just in the ingredients and the preparation of the wreath, but in what the two characters believe hanging the wreath on their door will *do*.

As you map out the correspondences that have poetic or ritual significance for your characters and their cultures, you can also identify the specific *mechanism* or *act* by which these correspondences are put to use magically. The wizard brewing a potion and our imagined artisan crafting stained glass for a moon temple offer us two such examples. For a third, perhaps your character knits a magical scarf, selecting threads with specific colors for specific reasons, and imbuing them with specific scents. Perhaps a scarf of radiant reds and violets, imbued with scents of rose, jasmine, and honey, is intended to ignite the erotic passions of its wearer; another, blue as twilight and scented like a cool pond beneath tree shadows, is intended to soothe and calm its wearer.

Or maybe your magic user is a chef, like Tita cooking meals for her family in Laura Esquivel's novel *Like Water for Chocolate*, and all her recipes include a dash of magic. The night Tita cooks quail in *rose petal* sauce, her sister Gertrudis eats such a quantity of the delicious meal and becomes so hot with passion that she sweats pink, rose-scented sweat. She tries a shower to cool herself, but by that time she is already emitting so much sexual heat that the water evaporates before touching her skin, and then the shower curtain bursts into flames. Fleeing the burning shower, wet and stark naked, Gertrudis is swept into the saddle by a soldier on horseback and is carried away into the hills, stuffed full of quail and rose petals and inflamed with lust. That incident in *Like Water for Chocolate* features both riveting storytelling and a lovely, consistent, simple magic system based on correspondences and enacted in cooking. By adding ingredients that correspond to specific moods and desires (as rose petals correspond to erotic love), Tita fills the meals that she prepares with her own emotions and with her intent, so that *her* passion kindles a corresponding passion in others.

In my own series *The Dakotaraptor Riders*, a pack of nightwatchers braid straps of leather around the grips of their weapons, one strap signifying each of their sisters, each one a gift from that sister, dyed in her chosen hue:

> Midnight for Veroshka and violet for Violetta, the orange of flame for Sveta, green for Nadya... Katya was last, pressing into my hand a strap as yellow as her hair, and when I gave her my red, she kissed me. Barely daring to breathe, I braided the others' straps around my kopye, the way the other nightwatchers' lives would now be braided around my own... It is the presence of your pack that keeps your hand from slipping, keeps your grip strong and your breath steady as you spin the rod or slash with fire. With your kopye braided, your pack is always with you as you ride out, as you watch the night for threats, as you fight for our survival. I have braided the kopye every day since.
>
> STANT LITORE, *INCURSION*

A single strap of leather may break; a braid of many strands is strong. The braiding is, in effect, a spell of strength that each of the nightwatchers casts anew each morning.

Maybe in the story you're writing, your correspondences are geometrical in nature, and your wizard draws elaborate designs on the walls of a cliff, or your rockhound mage collects specific stones and then presses them into a cliff wall in a specific pattern, creating a magical mosaic. Whatever the case, correspondences often work by symbolically linking things that are *tangible* (like rose petals) to experiences or concepts that are *intangible* or more abstract (like falling in love).

Exercise 22

> Create a simple recipe for a potion or meal that is intended to have a magical effect, or design a decorative theme for a house where the decorations are intended to have magical effects. As you add each ingredient or instruction for the preparation of the meal, or as you add each detail about the decorative scheme for the house, think intentionally about the correspondences. For each ingredient, item, or detail, brainstorm two or three alternatives that might work in its place, two or three other items that also correspond to the effect or experience that the spellcaster wishes to create. In this way, you can swiftly create a rudimentary table of correspondences to inform your magic system.

Another, quite different but still correspondences-driven mechanics of magic is at play in the Nickelodeon series *Avatar: The Last Airbender*. In the world of *Avatar*, "benders" exist who are able to weave the elements in order to fight, heal, or build. There are airbenders, earthbenders, firebenders, and waterbenders in that world who show innate talent for working with one of the elements. The benders hone and practice their craft through forms of movement and meditation that resemble the martial arts of East Asia. Rather than cast a spell as Merlin, Gandalf, or some other Western mage might, a bender performs a *kata*, and rather than sorcerer and apprentice, we often follow the tale of sensei and student. Underlying the craft of bending are the correspondences, this time interpreted using the symbolic vocabularies of Eastern mysticism. We find fire correlated with power and fueled by fury or passion; water correlated with the heart and blood; air with the mind and spirit; earth with body and bone. Airbenders flit nomadically on the wind, dancing around an obstacle, while earthbenders stand solid, feet planted firmly on the ground, meeting anything that comes at them head-on. Firebenders learned their magic art from dragons, waterbenders from the moon and ocean spirits incarnated in two fish, airbenders from flying "air bison," and earthbenders from giant badger moles who tunnel through mountains. Waterbenders act with greatest power during the full moon, and cannot bend at all during a lunar eclipse. Firebenders act with unthinkable power when a comet blazes in flame across the sky, but they cannot access their abilities during a solar eclipse. Note the complementarity of this magic system. *Avatar* is about the play of opposites and about the human need to find balance amid turbulence. This concern for balance governs not only *Avatar*'s magic system, but also its ethics and its approach to character development. By learning from each other and by each bringing to the team specific strengths the others lack, we grow—and we grow safe and strong.

EVOCATION AND THAUMATURGY

Another approach to devising a mechanics of magic is neatly summarized in Jim Butcher's *The Dresden Files*, though Jim Butcher didn't invent it; it's an encapsulation or summary within a fantasy-novel context of how the magic systems of European lore operate (with a dash of West African magic added here and there). In *Storm Front*, the wizard and private investigator Harry Dresden tells Chicago police detective Karrin Murphy about two ways to wield magic. One is *evocation*, by which the wizard focuses their will to *evoke* a sudden and strong effect on the material world. They might, for example, send a blast of wind rushing down an alley, or heat up the air abruptly and fling a fireball at their opponent. Dresden calls evocation "quick and dirty magic"; it's flashy and great in combat, but also messy and potentially chaotic; magical tools (such as wands, staffs, and amulets) can be used to focus the wizard's intent and will specifically on the desired effect.

The other method, which requires preparation and great care with ingredients, is *thaumaturgy*, by which the mage makes something small occur in order to produce a similar result on something big. Just as correspondences link the tangible and the intangible, thaumaturgy links something small and symbolic with something larger that the smaller thing represents. Usually the link requires that some piece of the larger object is included in the smaller. Examples might include a drop of blood anointing a doll (which can then be used to heal, harm, or augment the person the doll represents) or a strand of hair added to a spell whose target is the individual from whose head that hair has been plucked.

Once Harry Dresden has laid out this framework for the reader, we can follow along as he performs diverse and varied feats of magic, because we understand the base mechanics of his system, the principles according to which his magic works. This specificity and grounding is particularly important for *The Dresden Files* because Harry Dresden is not a mystical magic worker but a mechanical one, a practitioner rather than a philosopher. Harry Dresden is the wizard who rolls up his sleeves, gets his hands dirty, and, at the end of the day, collects a paycheck from the Chicago police department and other clients for solving supernatural mysteries. Accordingly, Dresden explains how magic works with the same prosaic simplicity that a plumber or a carpenter might explain the basics of their trade.

SONGS AND NAMING

There are many other inventive ways to write the crafting and casting of spells into a story—in part because, as we have seen, there are different traditions of magic and magical lore around the world. Some traditions have nothing to do with assembling ingredients to create a potion, an enchanted glass window, or a doll. In Finland's national epic, the *Kalevala*, wielders of magic instead *sing* imagined effects and events into existence. If the old spell-singer Vainamoinen, traveling across the snow-covered tundra, needs firewood, he may sit down for a bit, set his hands on his knees, and *sing* of green life and growing, until improbable trees push from the soil and tower upward to scratch at the sky. If he gets lonely during the long arctic night, he might sing of a companion until one appears, either ghostly or material, to sit across from him at his fire.

J.R.R. Tolkien, an avid scholar and translator of the *Kalevala*, wrote a wizard's duel into *The Silmarillion*, in which the elven king Finrod Felagund battles the Dark Lord Sauron, each hurling spells at the other in the form of song:

> He [Sauron] chanted a song of wizardry,
> Of piercing, opening, of treachery,
> Revealing, uncovering, betraying.
> Then sudden Felagund there swaying
> Sang in answer a song of staying,
> Resisting, battling against power,
> Of secrets kept, strength like a tower,
> And trust unbroken, freedom, escape;
> Of changing and of shifting shape,
> Of snares eluded, broken traps,
> The prison opening, the chain that snaps.
> Backwards and forwards swayed their song.

> J.R.R. TOLKIEN, *THE SILMARILLION*

Isn't that beautiful? Sauron sings a song of uncovering and revealing in order to strip Finrod's disguise; Finrod responds with a song of secrets kept and chains snapped. Their contest is fought with words, with competing narratives about what is about to occur or about what could occur. In Middle-earth, spellcraft is *literally* storycraft. The best storyteller wins; their spell is the one that has final effect.

During his lifetime, Tolkien witnessed fascist dictators come to power within the democracies they would later abolish, accumulating support by means of their oratory, weaving spells over their listeners, seducing citizens with stories in which the voters were cast simultaneously as victims and as incipient heroes. The most compelling storyteller is the one who gets to shape the nation's identity and future. No wonder Finrod and Sauron battle by telling opposing stories. Similarly, in Tolkien's *The Two Towers*, the wizard Saruman's most dangerous magic is the power of his voice. For Tolkien, the real magic is rhetoric, and spellcraft is a matter of naming and renaming, describing and redescribing. Sauron, in *The Lord of the Rings*, is out to rename himself and describe himself as the god of Middle Earth. His defeat at the hands of the hobbits is the result of a failure of imagination. There was no place for hobbitish humility, compassion, and earthiness in Sauron's grand tale of power and conquest; he could not *understand* the hobbits, and so he could not predict Frodo and Sam's journey to destroy the Ring, nor anticipate their choice not to wield the Ring as a weapon.

In other fictional magic systems, the power to define, describe, and change a thing rests in knowing and *naming* it. For Ursula K. Le Guin magic requires learning the true identities of things. Only when we see and name a thing as it truly is, are we then able to summon it to our aid. To learn magic in *A Wizard of Earthsea*, Ged Sparrowhawk must memorize the "true names" of things, and seek to understand them. He must learn to name things as they are, not as how he wants or perceives them to be:

"What must I do to make that diamond remain diamond? How is the changing-spell locked, and made to last?"

The Master Hand looked at the jewel that glittered on Ged's palm, bright as the prize of a dragon's hoard. The old Master murmured one word, *"Tolk,"* and there lay the pebble, no jewel but a rough grey bit of rock. The Master took it and held it out on his own hand. "This is a rock; *tolk* in the True Speech," he said, looking mildly up at Ged now. "A bit of the stone of which Roke Island is made, a little bit of the dry land on which men live. It is itself. It is part of the world. By the Illusion-Change you can make it look like a diamond—or a flower or a fly or an eye or a flame—" The rock flickered from shape to shape as he named them, and returned to rock. "But that is mere seeming. Illusion fools the beholder's senses; it makes him see and hear and feel that the thing is changed. But it does not change the thing. To change this rock into a jewel, you must change its true name. And to do that, my son, even to so small a scrap of the world, is to change the world. It can be done. Indeed it can be done. It *is* the art of the Master Changer, and you will learn it, when you are ready to learn it. But you must not change one thing, one pebble, one grain of sand, until you know what good and evil will follow on that act."

URSULA K. LE GUIN,
A WIZARD OF EARTHSEA

Lore (meaning knowledge) and understanding are the requirements for magic in Earthsea. For spellcraft to work, it is necessary to know a thing's true name, to know its nature, what part of the world it is, and thus to know what would occur if it were removed or altered.

With less care and caution, the young sorceress Sybel in Patricia McKillip's novel *The Forgotten Beasts of Eld* dreams of keeping her own menagerie of the most ancient, unique, and mystical creatures, from a dragon to a great white bird flying high over distant forests. She ransacks ancient grimoires and tomes of forgotten lore in search of the name and nature of each of these creatures. Only then can she call their name in the night, calling again and again until the creature responds and takes wing to come find her. Sybel must learn each creature in order to summon it.

Or consider the "magic" that Meg Murray wields against the universe-destroying Echthroi in Madeleine L'Engle's novel *A Wind in the Door*. When your opponent's goal is to subtract living beings from creation, then it becomes an act of resistance to name and assert their existence and their unique value and presence in the universe, to fill the emptiness with their presence and with your love for them:

> I Name you, Echthroi. I Name you Meg.
> I Name you Calvin.
> I Name you Mr. Jenkins.
> I fill you with Naming.
> Be!
> Be, butterfly and behemoth,
> be galaxy and grasshopper,
> star and sparrow,
> you matter,
> you are,
> be!
> Be, caterpillar and comet,
> be porcupine and planet,

sea sand and solar system
sing with us,
dance with us,
rejoice with us,
for the glory of creation,
angle worms and angel host,
chrysanthemum and cherubim
(O cherubim)
Be!

MADELEINE L'ENGLE, *A WIND IN THE DOOR*

Meg's song of Naming is much like the song-battle between Finrod and Sauron; Meg's task is to imagine and speak the value and worth, the identity and the name, of herself and of other beings—even ones, like the school principal Mr. Jenkins, whom she had previously loathed. Meg's task is to *love*. Remember Exercise 5 in Chapter 1, when I asked what the ultimate magic and the ultimate reason for magic might be, in your created world? For Madeleine L'Engle, love is the ultimate magic.

Exercise 23

Wizard in English means *wise one*. Many of the fictional wizards we are most familiar with—from Gandalf to Ged, from Harry Potter to Harry Dresden—are either scholars or students. There is a lot they have to learn in order to work magic. In actual cultural magic systems in our own world, a Celtic shaman would need to have learned the correspondences and have spells ready to recite, a Norse witch would need to be able to read the runes, and a Yoruba seer in the Caribbean would need to know the names and the natures of the orishas, so that she could consult the appropriate spirits to find her clients answers to their questions. Accordingly, one of the keys to unlocking your magic system—and its potential for storytelling—is to identify the *lore*, the knowledge needed in order to work magic. What knowledge do mages in your fictional world require, and how do they obtain it?

As an exercise, come up with a form of lore that can't be learned in a book. Maybe your world has no grimoires, no spellbooks. After all, in our own world, there have been fortune tellers who try to scry the future in the arrangements of tea leaves or in the entrails of slaughtered birds on an altar. Maybe your mage needs to have learned (at her grandmother's knee) a complex visual vocabulary of omens, so that if two ravens fly over her path, she knows immediately what it means. Maybe your mage needs to know the uses of every herb in the forest behind the trailer he lives in. Maybe your mage can make trees unroot themselves and walk across town, but only if they know the age of each tree, or only if they know which trees have rotten wood (and are thus susceptible to a spell) and which are strongly rooted and sound.

What lore do *your* mages need, and why? And what will make it especially difficult to get? What if your mage who would have learned a vocabulary of omens at her grandmother's knee ignored her grandmother, preferring to play video games, until it was too late, until her grandmother was dying and there was time left to learn only a little? What if your mage can make magical things happen on future dates by memorizing the position that the stars will have on those dates, but is slowly going blind? Get playful with the possibilities! What makes wizards knowledgeable in your world, and what makes them wise?

THE MAGIC OF IMPROBABILITY

Here's yet another route for designing a system of spellcraft, this time from Margaret Weis and Tracy Hickman's *Death Gate Cycle*. In that series, there are two godlike races—the Sartan and the Patryns—who wield magic to stunning effect, and who are capable not just of making a magical bird sing by a king's bed, but of creating and destroying entire worlds. Their magic is based on imagining improbabilities. Anything they can *imagine*, they can call into being by *speaking* it in the runes of their language:

> Reality is simply the manifestation of intersecting waves of possibility. It is a vast and almost incomprehensible weave of solid physics in the midst of a myriad of infinite potentials. Science, technology, and biology all use the woven rope of reality.
>
> Magic, on the other hand, functions by reweaving the fabric of reality. A wizard begins by concentrating on the wave of probabilities rather than on reality itself. Through his learning and his powers, he looks out upon the myriad waves of infinite possibilities to find that part of the wave where his desired reality would be true. Then the wizard creates a harmonic wave of possibility to bend the existing wave so that what was once only possible becomes part of what is true. In this way the magician weaves his desire into existence.
>
> For example, a wizard stands on a field of battle against a great knight. The spell caster, wearing only his robes, is at the mercy of the armored and more powerful knight. This is reality and, if left alone, the knight will most likely slay the wizard without much resistance. However, the wizard

knows from his study where the possibility (desired effect) of a protective shield exists on one of the countless waves of possibility. The wizard sets up a harmonic wave of possibility through his motions, thoughts, words, signs, and other aides. This magic alters the possibility wave so that what was once the possibility of a magical shield is woven into reality. The new reality includes the desired effect, and so the magical shield now guards the wizard.

Although, to the outside observer, the protective field seems to spring up around the wizard from nothing, it would be more accurate to say that the possibility of such a field has been called into reality from the infinite possibilities...

MARGARET WEIS AND TRACY HICKMAN,
DRAGON WING

In other words, like Finrod and Sauron, the wizard literally sings about something that is possible, until it becomes true. But the more improbable the possibility, the greater the effort. It is possible that the knight's horse might stumble over a jagged rock and toss its rider from the saddle, and this isn't too improbable, so it would be an easier spell to cast. It is also possible that a wizard might suddenly have a shield (though less likely). It is even *possible* that a dragon could swoop down and sear the knight from existence before he can smite the wizard (but this is *much* less likely, requiring more complex magic to make it happen).

In the *Death Gate Cycle*, the vocabulary of spellcraft consists of the runes themselves, which the Patryns and the Sartan articulate in a magical language, stringing these sigils and symbols together into spells, just as you and I string words and concepts together to create sentences. The Sartan do this by singing and dancing the runes, the Patryns by writing the runes into their bodies, tattooed in their flesh.

Exercise 24

Write down a quick list of what spells are easy to cast in your magic system or what magical effects are easier to achieve, and what effects are *difficult* to achieve. And write down *why*. What makes a spell easy to cast for your mages, and what makes a spell hard? For Weis and Hickman's Patryns and Sartan, the difficulty is determined by how improbable the effect of the spell would be. For the warlock Roderick Burgess in Neil Gaiman's *The Sandman*, summoning one of the Endless is difficult because the ingredients for such a ritual are very difficult to obtain. For Sybel in Patricia McKillip's *The Forgotten Beasts of Eld*, acquiring the magical creature you desire is difficult because the creature is all but forgotten, and the knowledge needed to locate and summon it is difficult to find. You can also play with the reader's (and the mage's) expectations regarding the ease or difficulty of a spell. Gandalf the Grey, in J.R.R. Tolkien's *The Lord of the Rings*, casts increasingly complex spells of opening, calling to mind every such spell that he has ever studied, each spell he can remember, and he still isn't able to open the door to the Mines of Moria—because the doors only respond to the very simplest of all passwords: the word *friend*.

In the magic system you are developing or refining for your own story, what spells are easy, what spells are difficult, and why? Write that down, and then think of 1-2 examples of cases in which your magic user might either think that a spell will be easy and then find it much harder than they expected, or think that it will be hard and find it to be surprisingly simple (like the password to Moria). Such moments when our expectations get flipped upside down are a lot of fun, and they prevent your magic system from operating within your story merely as a restrictive rule set. Moments when what happens is not what we expect keep us guessing and keep your story, well, magical.

WHEN SPELLS FAIL

When designing the mechanics of spellcraft, it's important to also consider the question: When *doesn't* it work? What causes magic to fail? Perhaps random chance—it could be fun to have a story in which spells only work six out of every seven times. That seventh time (when the spell fizzles) could occur at the most inconvenient moments. Or perhaps it is a lack of skill. Perhaps your mage is young, and magic is very hard. Paul Atreides initially fails to use the Voice effectively in *Dune*, as he is still early in his training. (I know that diligent SF readers may argue that the Voice doesn't count as *magic*, but it operates like magic and the Bene Gesserit are seen as witches by the other characters, and the same storytelling logic applies.) Perhaps a spell will fizzle or backfire dangerously if the ingredients tossed into the cauldron aren't *just right*. Maybe your wizard needs a certain magic weed (insert marijuana and LSD jokes here), but magic weed isn't regulated by any government agency, and different suppliers provide magic weed of differing qualities and concentrations. Possibly, your wizard intended to use 20 milligrams of magic and got 45 instead, with either explosive or psychedelic effects. Or perhaps spells are powered by faith, and the mage or cleric who truly trusts that the mountain will move because she tells it to will see that mountain move, but the mage who doubts or loses her confidence for a moment can't maintain the spell. You can find exhilarating opportunities for storytelling when you consider not only how to make the spells work but how to make them *not* work.

Exercise 25

What *foils* a mage in your fictional world? What causes a spell to fizzle? What causes it to backfire? Knowing what you know so far about the source and function of your mage's power and abilities, write down a list of possible things that could go wrong in casting a spell. Which of these possibilities strike you as especially compelling or entertaining? Can you write down three different scenes, scenarios, or incidents when a spell could go wrong in that particular way? For example, if you are casting a spell to fill a glass with drinkable liquid, a misfired spell might have different effects and different stakes depending on whether you are watering your houseplants, giving a toast at a wedding, or trying to survive a trek across a desert. And it might produce a different scene depending on the nature of the misfire: Does the glass raised in a toast simply remain empty, or does every glass in the room turn into a fountain like an uncorked champagne bottle, spraying the entire wedding party? Brainstorm the possibilities for misfired magic in *your* story.

Exercise 26

What *exhausts* a mage in your fictional world? Think through this, perhaps more specifically than you have before. The specific manner in which your mage becomes too weary to cast another spell, and the specific reason why they become so, reveals a lot about how magic works in your imagined world and what it *means*. Gandalf's exhaustion after holding a door shut against the Balrog's approach in *The Fellowship of the Ring* is a severe mental fatigue; he has had to call spell after spell to mind out of dusty memory, and then speak them with the full force of his will. His strain is intensified by fear: he has encountered a will as strong as his own, an opposing will that nearly broke him. What if an enemy's story of who they are and what they can do is stronger than your own?

Raistlin, in *Dragonlance*, wearies after casting several strong spells because of the wrenching impact this casting has on his physical body; he coughs up blood. For Raistlin, magic is a ruthless prioritizing of mind over matter, brain over body, but he nonetheless remains imprisoned within his failing body, suffering its costs.

What wears out *your* wizard? What tires *your* witch? Earlier in this book, I asked you to consider what risks they run when they cast spells or wield magic. Now consider what those risks *mean*. Why does it cost them that? How does that express the themes of your story? What kind of cost is most relevant to the kind of story you are excited to tell? Is your story about the dichotomy between mind and body, or about the conflict between opposing narratives of what humanity could be, or about the destructiveness of addiction, or about something else? Come up with a strain on your magic user that is aligned with and expresses the thematic concerns of your tale.

TOOLS AND DEVICES

One of my favorite examples of a magic system with elegant mechanics appears in M. H. Boroson's novel *The Girl with the Ghost Eyes*, this time based on the Daoshi magic of China. In the novel, Li-lin, the daughter of a Daoishi exorcist in 1898 Chinatown, San Francisco, needs to travel into the spirit world to search for someone who is lost there. To do this, Li-lin first writes symbols on paper, creating a spiritual passport with the lost man's name on it, so that if she gives it to him, he can come back; then she burns it, so that the passport will exist in the spiritual world. She takes up a peachwood sword (because *peachwood* can harm spirits) and ties a red cord around her wrist so that she can follow the cord back to her body. Then she crosses over. The magic is wondrous, easy to follow, and exciting in the opportunities it creates for plot, because as readers, we are shown immediately that going into the spirit world is dangerous, and if any of those three devices (passport, peachwood sword, red cord) should be lost, we know Li-lin may be in a lot of trouble.

Many other cultures have also chosen *fire* as the mechanism for travel from the physical to the spiritual world. What is immolated in our world appears in the other; the smoke we see rising into the sky suggests the intangibility of the spiritual world, as if by changing into smoke, what has burned is traveling into that world of mist. Thus, the funeral rites of Scandinavian kings and queens on their burning ships, sailing out of this world so that they can go viking across the dark waters of the next.

Bronze Age Mediterranean cultures, however, simply left items with the dead unburned, because what is sealed up with the dead will be present with them in the other world. In Greece, coins on the eyes will pay for the boatman to ferry a soul across the river between life and death; in Egypt, grave goods ensure that the dearly departed will have food and drink and items of luxury on the other side.

Coins on the eyes, a paper passport in the fire, shredded lace and pages from a romance novel mixed with tequila—magic is most compelling when it is very tangible. The wizard's spellcraft suggests that one might be able to control the big intangibilities of human experience (love, life, death, good and bad luck, disease and healing) by precise action taken with small, tangible, controllable items. Maybe it is for that reason that magical tools and devices—like the paper passport and the peachwood sword—hold our attention as readers.

What tools do *your* mages require? Rather than Li-lin's peachwood sword and ghostly passport, what items and devices does your magic user carry with them into danger? When brainstorming such tools (and finding the opportunities they present for ramping up the excitement in your story), consider multiple possible needs they might fulfill:

DEFENSE

Amulets of protection are a classic example. I love the use of the amulet Ethel carries with her in the Netflix adaptation of Neil Gaiman's *The Sandman*. The amulet's use is certainly disturbing; when someone attacks its wearer, they are ripped apart. Nor can old age harm the wearer; Ethel has lived for over a century. But then she is confronted with a dilemma, when she believes that the only way she can save her son is to give him the amulet instead, preserving his life while dying almost immediately of her own extreme old age. The scene when she places the amulet around her son's neck, cries, and asks his forgiveness for having been a terrible mother to him, is unforgettable storytelling.

FOCUS

In Jim Butcher's *Dresden Files*, Harry Dresden's wand is a device for making sure the fire he evokes in midair shoots in one direction, rather than burning down the entire building around him (which, nevertheless, does tend to happen). Similarly, the weapons in Rooster Teeth's animated series *RWBY*, elaborately designed and unique to each character, are tools to focus and channel each character's "aura," their spiritual and magical energy. In their world, where elite, trained huntsmen and huntresses venture outside their kingdoms to battle monsters that would otherwise devour humanity, each character's weapon is an expression of themselves and an extension of their natural abilities. While the characters themselves aren't mages, their weapons are powered by Dust, a magical substance that permits extraordinary effects.

RELIC

In some cases, a magical artifact or device might be carried only secondarily as a tool; its primary purpose might be that of an heirloom or sacred relic. Variations on this occur when your character needs to either protect, conceal, or destroy the magical device they carry. Frodo must keep the Ring hidden and endure the devastating psychological effects it has on him, until he can destroy it; Harry Potter and team must keep the Horcruxes they have found out of enemy hands. Possibly your character is bearing a device that has a demon, monster, or dark god sealed away inside it; their task may be to protect the item and *never break it open*. Or perhaps someone has stolen your character's relic, and your character's task is to rush across a continent or across oceans of time to *get it back*.

TRANSPORTATION

Needless to say, an enchanted flying car or a magic carpet or a sleigh pulled by eight or nine flying reindeer also makes a compelling magical device and one that, though it can't be dropped into a pocket (or can it?), *can* be stolen, just as smaller devices can. And it can have its own constraints. Perhaps a carpet can only be ridden by the pure of heart, or reindeer only fly on Christmas Eve, or an enchanted pickup truck's fuel tank be filled only by singing country music into it. One can even love a vehicle or name it. Or fear it; young Theodora Veronica Claus, Santa's daughter, may be eager for Christmas because she wants to bring joy or solace to children around the world, especially to the impoverished, the orphaned, or the abused, and she wants to place toys at the hearth or under the tree so badly she aches with that yearning, but she is simultaneously, mortally terrified of flight.

You can also have a great deal of fun creating the lore behind a given magical device. How was it created, or where was it found? King Arthur carries a magical sword because someone sheathed it in a rock and left the message that whoever pulled it out would be the rightful king of England, or because a woman in white samite lifted the blade from the waters of an enchanted lake and blessed his reign. Seeking to ensure his resurrection, Voldemort created his Horcruxes by means of murder, splitting off and sealing away pieces of his soul. The One Ring was forged inside a volcano. Just as most superheroes and many mages have origin stories, magical devices might have them, too.

But perhaps the single most useful question of all is, *What effect does this tool have on my character?* Our devices shape us, as much as we shape them. Consider how much a smartphone carried in the pocket shapes our lives, and the way we communicate with people, and how we use our time. How much more might this be true of a magical tool? The device's effect might be malign or perilous, as in the case of the One Ring and its slow, persistent corruption of its wearer, or of the AURYN in *The Neverending Story*, each use of which costs a memory. Or the device's effect might be one of reshaping perspective; perhaps that magical amulet allows the wearer to hear others' thoughts, or translates other languages—not only other *human* languages, but the languages of cricket and screech owl and snake in the grass, the quiet gossip of rabbits under the hedge, and the ancient speech of root and rock, sand and stone. The magical brooch in Lloyd Alexander's novel *The Black Cauldron* allows its wearer to perceive everything more vividly, detecting the track of forest animals, hearing every sound in the wood, seeing the sunlight on every leaf, so that, from the perspective of others, the wearer has an observation and an insight denied to most. Or perhaps your magical device lets your mage or magician's apprentice see spiritual and magical beings that are invisible to all others, so that the character is always talking to people who don't appear to be there. Or the device might be a "crutch," a magical key that allows the user to perform spells or that amplifies their beginner abilities to an expert level; but as long as they rely on the device, they cease honing their own native talents. Maybe the creature imprisoned within or inhabiting a magical device is no demon or dark god, but a being that the protagonist falls in love with. Maybe your character must give up the very device that has granted them magic, breaking it open to set free the one they love.

Exercise 27

Come up with a magical device, and pair either its use, its relinquishment, or its destruction with some cost. The cost should be quite high, from your character's perspective. Now come up with a scenario where they might need to willingly use, relinquish, or destroy the item. What options can you brainstorm that lead to the most difficult and heartwrenching choices for the character, and thus the most exciting possible story for the reader?

DUELS

When I was a child, Walt Disney's *The Sword in the Stone* taught me that a wizards' duel is an opportunity for imaginative play, and that it is won by the mage who demonstrates the greatest imagination and cunning. In the movie, Merlin and Mad Madam Mim transform into various creatures—hare and alligator, deer and dragon—but Merlin, even after being gulped down by a hungry firedrake, achieves victory in the end by transforming into an organism that can destroy Mim from the inside—a germ.

How I delighted in that duel, in its spectacle, its humor, its suspense, and its inventiveness! Later, as an adolescent, I devoured any fantasy films I could find on VHS tapes at our local ma and pop movie shop. (This was before the rise and subsequent demise of Blockbuster Video, and certainly long before the advent of the DVD or of streaming video.) Such films were few and far between. There were a few that ignited the imagination—*The Neverending Story* and *Dragonslayer*—but most were just dreadful. I loved the stirring, braying music of *Wizards of the Lost Kingdom*, but the script was a hot mess, and the climactic wizards' duel was so disappointing that I turned off the credits afterward in a huff and went immediately to find pen and paper and write one of my own. In that movie, the villain and the child-mage hero had stood on top of two towers chucking colored lights at each other, back and forth, making use of the kind of special effects that the 1980s afforded. Two decades later, watching the *Harry Potter* films at the cinema with some curiosity as to what the director of a fantasy movie might do with the special effects of a later age, I found to my dismay that the clash of colored lights from *Wizards of the Lost Kingdom* was back. It looked prettier this time, but there was no creativity and fun to the duel. (In fairness to the *Harry Potter* films, conflicts with lesser villains and henchmen actually proved more interesting, at least in terms of spectacle, as many of these brief duels involved the environment, with shattered windows and glass slicing through the air and characters crashing into shelves, and such.)

The wizards' duel in Peter Jackson's film adaptation of *The Fellowship of the Ring* was more interesting, and made some choices I hadn't seen before. Gandalf and Saruman face off early in the film, these two wizened old men in wizard's robes with wizard's staffs, one staff gnarled and wooden, the other metallic and sharp. They wield their implements like quarterstaffs, and though neither staff connects with an opponent's body, their impact is nonetheless physical; Saruman swings his staff, and Gandalf flips in the air, slamming into the floor to bloody his face. Gandalf thrusts *his* staff out abruptly, and Saruman crumples as if he has been tripped. There are no flashy lights or sparkles; the magic is invisible but its effects are brutal, physical, and raw. Where wisdom and foresight have failed, we are left watching two old men beat the stuffing out of each other. With magic.

The scene took some lessons from *Star Wars* (even as the *Star Wars* films took lessons from Tolkien's fiction). In

The Empire Strikes Back, a well-paced and vivid lightsaber duel gives way to a war of magic, as Darth Vader steps back and, invisibly, rips pieces of equipment out of the walls and furniture off the floor to send hurtling toward his opponent. The key to an exciting duel or combat, as with any action scene, is improvisation and surprise. There need to be things that characters can crash into or be thrown through, as when Luke is sucked through a broken window, and there need to be items that can be turned into improvised weapons. Mages may fight with spells, but the mage who is fleeing her opponent may simply use a quick spell to chuck a rotary telephone or a lamp behind her to delay her pursuer. To make it more magical, more playful, perhaps the telephone transforms into a flock of bats midair, so that the pursuer flings up his arm across his face with a startled cry, losing both momentum and composure. (What will your fugitive mage do then? Turn back to the battle, getting in a quick blow while her chiropterophobic pursuer is alarmed and distracted? Or make good on her getaway?) Or perhaps the telephone crashes into the doorjamb by the pursuer's head, and after the pursuer has passed, that broken phone metamorphoses into a furious Rottweiler who leaps after the assailant mage, so that the pursuer becomes the pursued. The pursuer turns, eyes widening as he sees this slavering dog leaping at his face. What spell is cast then? Does he sweep a staff upward to knock the dog from the air? Do ten cornstalks suddenly sprout from the floor, improvising a fence, though one of limited efficacy? Does he freeze time? What does he *do*?

So a good duel or combat scene entails creative improvisation—and surprise after surprise after surprise.

That's what makes it fun. That's what makes it exciting. That's what makes it unforgettable.

This is true even if the duel doesn't involve *action* in the sense in which we usually think of action. In Neil Gaiman's *The Sandman*, Morpheus and a lord of hell (Lucifer in the televised adaptation, a lesser duke in the comic) each attempt to project their conjurings into the mind and the reality of their opponent—much like Finrod and Sauron in *The Silmarillion*.

"I am a dire wolf!" Lucifer gloats.

"I am a hunter," Morpheus retorts, "horse-riding, wolf-stabbing." On screen, the hunter hurls a javelin, and Lucifer hunches over, clutching a wound in her abdomen, her hand suddenly crimson with blood. It is Merlin and Mad Madam Mim again, each magic user trying to outwit and out-*imagine* the other. In homage to the childhood film, Lucifer even tries Merlin's gambit, declaring herself a "butcher bacterium, warm life destroying," but Morpheus responds by becoming a world, life-*nurturing*. And on they go, until the Sandman, at the end of the universe, becomes the one thing that can never be killed. Hope.

Morpheus's competition with Lucifer is beautifully written, and it is magical for all the same reasons that my *first* wizard's duel experience was magical, in *The Sword in the Stone*. In Gaiman's hands the mages' duel becomes especially meaningful, an imaginative expression and emotional exploration of his story's theme. For Gaiman, a car chase is never *just* a car chase, a duel is never *just* a duel: it's also the chance to tell a story.

Exercise 28

Write a wizards' duel. What is a magical combat like, in *your* story, using *your* magic system? How does it work, and how is it won? Is it to be won by endurance, by courage, by faith, by love, by strength, or by cunning? What does both the duel and the manner of conducting it reveal about magic, about what's important in your story, and about the types of choices your character is willing to make?

Rituals

There is a gorgeous moment in Season 1, Episode 4 of Amazon's *The Rings of Power* in which Elrond Half-Elven, an outsider, witnesses a ritual deep underground in the mountain kingdom of Khazad-dum. After the collapse of a mine traps four dwarven workers, Princess Disa of the Dwarves sings a chant that is heartrending in its beauty, her voice filling the underground halls and chambers as the voices of a choir might fill a cathedral. When she falls silent at last, the mountain shifts, rumbling. Asked by Elrond what she was singing, Disa tells him she was asking the mountain to move, to preserve the lives of her trapped kindred.

This is beautiful (and economical) storytelling for several reasons. First, the ritual is seen through the eyes of an outsider, who can ask uninformed questions on behalf of the reader, and who can model for us how moving the ritual is. As we see Elrond moved, we feel moved too, even before we understand what the ritual was for. Second, the ritual is a larger-scale expression of a magic system that we have witnessed previously on a small scale; the dwarves mine by singing to the mountain, resonating the stone. We have seen their children taught nursery rhymes whose rhythms rearrange rock. Now we see their princess pleading with the mountain for the lives of her people. In both scope and emotional impact, it is the largest dwarven "spell" we have witnessed; hearing it, we are overtaken with wonder, and we become more invested in the dwarves and their story. Third, the ritual reveals to us things about the dwarven culture that we had previously suspected and now *see*: their communal nature, their deep attachment to each other (no dwarf left behind!), and their kinship and close feeling for the mountain, which to them is a living thing.

A spell can be a hasty thing, like casting Fireball in a D&D campaign, or, as we have seen, it can be something that requires some preparation and gathering of ingredients. A *ritual* is the least hasty magic of all. It may have multiple participants. It may have an audience. It may need to occur at a specific time or place. It may be very risky, especially if you botch the rite. The mountain, after all, may crush the dwarves instead of freeing them when it moves. A ritual may be fraught with religious or other personal meaning for the mage. For all these reasons, the excitement of writing a ritual is that a ritual is a story expressed through action. It's a story about who the participants are, what they desire, and what they're willing to do to get it. And because rituals are a repeated thing, in some cases passed down through centuries, a ritual is also the story of a people, as Disa's rite is implicitly a story of the dwarves, what they care about and who they are, sung in their moment of grave peril.

Your magic workers may be summoning and caging an otherworldly creature, performing a sacred dance or seance in which they are possessed by spiritual beings, or holding hands and singing their desire for the sky to rain. Consider: What rituals are written into your fictional magic system? When might certain rituals be called for? Are they performed often, or rarely? What do those rituals mean? What does it mean to your characters to take part in them? Is your character leading the ritual, or are they crying tears of joy because this is the first time they have ever been permitted to take part, and they have waited so long to join in this act of healing or preserving or feeding their people by magic?

What is the purpose of the ritual you have in mind? Is it the binding of two souls (for love or other reasons)? Is it an exorcism? A healing? A bit of magical weaponcraft? The cleansing of a house, either cleansing a new home or cleansing a home after a crisis (that's what witches have brooms for, after all)? Is it the opening of a portal between worlds? A bestowing of magic on a new, fledgling mage? What items and devices are used in the ritual, and does it feel timeless and ancient (as rituals often do)? Or does it feel fresh, an old thing transformed and made new? In Leslie Marmon Silko's novel *Ceremony*, a Navajo medicine man explains why, when he performs the same rites of healing his ancestors did, *his* ceremony makes use of contemporary items that didn't exist back when his ancestors lived:

"There are some things I have to tell you," Betonie began softly. "The people nowadays have an idea about the ceremonies. They think the ceremonies must be performed exactly as they have always done, maybe because one slip-up or one mistake and the whole ceremony must be stopped and the sand painting destroyed. That much is true. They think that if a singer tampers with any part of the ritual, great harm can be done, great power unleashed." He was quite for a while, looking up at the sky through the smoke hole. "That much can be true also. But long ago when the people were given these ceremonies, the changing began, if only in the aging of the yellow gourd rattle or the shrinking of the skin around the eagle's claw, if only in the different voices from generation to generation, singing the chants. You see, in many ways, the ceremonies have always been changing... Things which don't shift and grow are dead things. They are things the witchery people want. Witchery works to scare people, to make them fear growth. But it has always been necessary, and more than ever now, it is. Otherwise we won't make it. We won't survive. That's what the witchery is counting on: that we will cling to the ceremonies they way they were, and then their power will triumph, and the people will be no more."

LESLIE MARMON SILKO, *CEREMONY*

In Silko's *Ceremony*, the way that the ceremony is changing and *why* speaks directly to the themes of the book, to the things the protagonist must learn if he is to heal and survive, the things his people must learn if they are to heal and survive: *"Things which don't shift and grow are dead things."* The ritual is meaningful because it enacts the story the characters are living; it makes that story real to their eyes, and it shows the reader what that story means, why it matters.

Go and do likewise.

In your own writing, as you create a magic system and as you design its mechanics—its methods and its rules (and which can be bent and which can be broken), its parameters and its practices, its recipes and its spells—also consider what rituals may be important to the mages in your story, and what rituals may occur during the story to help your characters make the transition from *who they were* to *who they need to be*.

Toni Morrison's *Beloved* ended with an exorcism; romantic comedies for centuries have ended with a wedding (or with the expectation of one). *Star Wars* (the 1976 film) ended with a victory celebration and the conferral of medals of valor. If your story were to end with a ceremony—and, specifically, with an explicitly *magical* ceremony—what would it be like, and in what ways would you use that ritual to invite the reader into celebrating your story and what matters most in it? Something to think about.

5 | THE ETHICS OF MAGIC

THE USE OF MAGIC MIGHT BE CRUEL OR KIND, or both at once. Magic, at its core, involves either exerting one's will upon the world or acting as the channel through which some other potent force—a god; a demon; the elemental forces of creation, destruction, order, or chaos; or simply the community as a united whole—exerts its will upon the world. Our every action—each act of compassion and each act of cruelty—changes our world. Magic is a way of intensifying or speeding up that change, that impact. (Remember the example I used in Chapter 3, where in one fictional world, a witch is labeled a *swift*, because of the rapidity and force of her impact on her world?) Because of that intensified impact, the use of magic immediately raises ethical questions or implies things about the ethics of your story and its characters, and how they see their responsibility to others.

So, here are a few questions for a storyteller to consider:

- What are *your* ethical positions, and how are these implicitly written into your fictional world?

- Are their *rules* or *laws* by which the inhabitants of your fictional world express and attempt to enforce an ethics of magic?

- How do your characters *feel* if they use magic (whether purposefully or accidentally) in a way that they regard as unethical or harmful? (This could have quite an impact on their future choices and character development.)

IDENTIFYING YOUR ETHICS

You don't necessarily need to articulate an entire system of ethics, but you should know what ethical positions are important to you and how the magic system you are using interacts with, implies, or (possibly) gets in the way of your ethics. It needn't be complex, only clear; your position might be something as simple as the Golden Rule from the New Testament (*do unto others as you would have them do unto you*). The Threefold Law in Wicca applies that type of ethical position to the use of magic in a way that is scarcely less simple but that is nevertheless profound: *What you do comes back to you threefold.* (Thus, in Wicca, *do what ye will, an it harm none,* remembering that the good you put into the world revisits you, but the evil revisits you, too, and returns to you larger than when it departed.)

One of Terry Pratchett's characters defines *evil* as the act of using another person as a *thing,* an object; "that's always how it starts." Magic might provide many opportunities to treat people as things. What happens when you discover that you can use another person as an object? What does that *do* to your mage—to their psychology, their character?

Peter Parker, who becomes Spiderman, is told by his ill-fated uncle that *with great power comes great responsibility*. What do you personally believe about the responsibilities you have, or don't have, for exercising your own talents and abilities? Whether you perceive your own talents as great or humble, mighty or meager, skilled or apprenticelike makes little difference to this question, which is: In any situation in which you have skill or ability that could have impact on others, what responsibilities do you have? And how do *your* beliefs about this, how do *your* ethical convictions seep into the thinking of your characters?

J. K. Rowling's Hogwarts is certainly playful, but I could never get into the story the way many readers did; its magic, though evocative, usually appeared to be unmoored from any conscience or ethical convictions. Harry could make an abusive aunt swell up like a balloon and float away over the city, but he never appeared to *feel* anything, one way or the other, about having done so. Medical professionals in our world take the Hippocratic oath, promising to do no harm. The young witches and wizards of Hogwarts don't appear to have any oath of their own or any code of conduct, other than school dress codes and curfews and three magical curses that are expressly forbidden (mind control, torture, and murder). That leaves a world of ethical gray area that is dipped into but never really commented on in the books.

The wizards' school I grew up with was the school on Roke, in Ursula K. Le Guin's *A Wizard of Earthsea*, where the teachers communicate both the empowering idea that their students will dare and achieve incredible things, and the rather daunting warning that you must consider the *effects* of those things before you attempt them:

> "It can be done. Indeed it can be done… But you must not change one thing, one pebble, one grain of sand, until you know what good and evil will follow on that act."

> URSULA K. LE GUIN,
> *A WIZARD OF EARTHSEA*

Le Guin's personal ethics, echoing throughout her fiction, is grounded in social responsibility and intentionality (thus, the concern for the consequences of one's actions). What is yours grounded in? What would *you* teach the young spellcasters, if you were a teacher at a magical academy?

Exercise 29

Answer the following questions (playfully and with thought) to start getting a more specific idea of what may underlie the ethics of your magic system:

- What would a responsible parent strive to teach a child who can use magic? What is this parent's favorite proverb or saying (repeated until the child can recite it before the parent even opens their mouth)?
- To whom or to what is your mage responsible? (Are they a cleric, answerable to a god? Are they like a sorcerous gunslinger, answerable to a code? Are they a veteran of magical conflicts who has "seen some shit,"

and they are answerable to the memory of a comrade, friend, or lover who died in their arms?)

- What magic must your character *never* do, and why?
- Consider the costs of magic. Who pays the cost, and how do you feel about that? (For example, what costs are paid by the mage themselves? Do they defer some costs to others, as in a ritual sacrifice?)

LAWS OF MAGIC

Accordingly, are there *rules* or *laws* of magic within your fictional world? In Harry Dresden's world, spells cast upon a human mind are illegal. So is necromancy. You can't mess with someone's mind, and you can't bring back the dead. Both offenses carry a death penalty.

In your fiction, are there worldly consequences for misuses of magic? Might a particular use of magic get a civilization crushed by the gods? Might a particular use of magic get the Magic Police knocking at one's door (or summon the attention of the Magic Gestapo, who don't bother to knock)? Might a particular use cause one's magic to wane or diminish? The moment you establish such consequences, you have material for *story*, because you can ask yourself, as the writer, both what consequences might be most terrifying to your mage, and what needs or passions might drive your mage to take such a risk—to act against their codes, and damn the consequences? To be swept along with a character who is making such high-stakes choices, who is risking it all, can be exhilarating for a reader.

MAGIC MISUSED

Finally, what do your characters feel about potential misuses of magic, especially their *own* misuses? For example, in *Avatar: The Last Airbender*, Aang is smitten with guilt and shame when his firebending gets his friend and love interest, Katara, burned. He vows never to practice firebending again. That can be a powerful story to tell, in which the young mage (or "bender," in the *Avatar* universe) is so appalled at the harm they have done that they turn away from that use of magic entirely. What is it that calls them back? What is it that might drive them or entice them to later do what they swore never again to do?

In the third season or "book" of *Avatar: The Last Airbender*, Aang confronts a specifically ethical dilemma: He is a pacifist, in fact the last surviving member of a culture that suffered genocide. Now he is called upon to save the world by battling and (presumably) slaying Fire Lord Ozai, who dreams of burning other races from the planet to make "breathing room" for his own people to spread and colonize. Aang doesn't question that Ozai *must* be stopped, nor that he is the one called upon to do it and who has the abilities necessary to do it. But his entire ethics is predicated on the conviction that life is sacred. He is vegetarian; his martial arts and use of magic is designed to evade and defuse, not to attack. Can he bring himself to kill? What will happen to the world if he does not? In conversation with one of his past selves, he is told that he must sacrifice his own spiritual and moral integrity to save the world. What will he choose? Or will he find a third way?

Less innocently than Avatar Aang, Willow in the television series *Buffy the Vampire Slayer* gets caught by her girlfriend, who realizes that Willow has been regularly editing her memory—a betrayal of her trust that is difficult to overstate. That misuse of magic costs Willow a romantic relationship and precipitates a story path down which Willow has to decide whether she will continue to use magic.

Exercise 30

What does the magic user in your story believe about their responsibilities toward others? Are they reluctant to use magic, or eager? What ethical dilemmas and personal choices might they be presented with? Devise a scenario in which the stakes are high—because people could get hurt, or because the mage could lose something they value, such as a relationship or a way home or a dream they've been pursuing—and examine that choice as a window into discovering your character more deeply, both what they feel and believe about magic, and what they feel and believe about themselves. What pushes them toward either choice? Where do they feel most torn? What if your mage has worked all their life to master magic, and now, to save others, they must commit an act that might deprive them of their magic forever? What if they must choose between saving a city and saving their beloved? What if they must choose between forgiving an abuser and ripping them apart? It is in our choices that we both become and discover who we really are.

Exercise 31

Come up with a law of magic and a reason your character might choose to break it. Maybe they break the law (or several laws!) for love? Now, write the defense your character makes after taking the stand in Magic Court. What does your enchanter have to say for themselves? When you read back over the defense speech you've written for them, what will you discover about their personality and their past, about why they made their choice, about their fears and desires, about the extent to which the law was just or unjust, about whether your character is remorseful or defiant, and about what magic really means to them?

When a character's personal ethics and their personal fears and desires collide, you have the potential for exciting storytelling, because exciting stories are all about the choices we make under pressure. Adding magic to a story is a way of increasing the pressure—and of putting characters in the position where they have the *power* to do things they may have longed to do but shouldn't, or the power to do things they have longed *not* to do but may believe they have the responsibility to do. Peter Parker, after all, decides *not* to intervene to prevent a burglary, and finds that the burglar ends up killing his beloved uncle. To whom is your fictional mage responsible, and for what, and what might drive them either to embrace or refuse their responsibilities at different times in the story? At what points will their choices under pressure make us wince, and what point will their choices make us cheer or pump our fists in the air?

6 | PULLING IT ALL TOGETHER: DESIGNING YOUR MAGIC SYSTEM

NOW YOU HAVE THE INGREDIENTS, and you can make something exciting and new, or something ancient but in a way that helps us see that lore and that magic vividly, as we never have before. *You* are the mage now, cooking a story in whatever cauldron you have found near at hand. What ingredients will you choose? What recipe will you brew? What effects do you most desire? Not even Merlin had access to the tools of craft you do, or could imagine half as many stories. Come! Your workshop awaits. Time to make something extravagant, creative, and wondrous.

Exercise 32

If it would be helpful to you, use the following worksheet to assemble your notes for designing your magic system.

What is magic?

What do your characters believe about the origin, purpose, and nature of magic in their world?

Costs

Environmental:

Personal:

Social:

Variable depending on source:

Culture

What are magic users *called*? (And do different people call them different things?

How do people feel about mages?

What roles do mages perform in the society?

To what degree is magic use *individual* or *communal*?

How is magic related to *mortality*?

Write down a legend of how magic came into the world:

Mechanics
In one sentence, how does magic work?
Notes on spells:

Notes on tools and magical devices:

Notes on rituals:

When does magic *not* work?

What exhausts a magic user?

If there was a duel or contest between magic users, what would it look like?

Ethics

What ethical positions of your own are written, implicitly or explicitly, into the fictional world of your story?

Does the mage in your story see a relationship between *magic* and *compassion*, between *magic* and *justice*, between *magic* and *love*, or between *magic* and *creating*? How does this perspective inform what uses they think magic *should* be put to?

What must a magic user *never* do, and why?

Are there laws of magic? What are they? What happens if they're broken?

In what ways might your character be tempted to *misuse* magic?

Sample recipe and instructions for a magical spell, with your notes on what this recipe reveals about the magic system you're designing:

Your character's impassioned defense in Magic Court after breaking one (or several) of the laws of magic, for love (see Exercise 31):

There! These worksheets are simple ones, but they do allow you to collect in one place each of the most important ingredients for the potion or brew that will be your magic system, which you will then use (hopefully with wondrous effects) in the magic rite that is your storycraft, your creation of a work of fiction we have never read or heard before and that we may never forget.

Now that you have these ingredients, start mixing! Consider how the things you have learned about your magic system might play out in different scenes, different storylines. What opportunities for plot does your unique magic system create? What pressures does it place on each of your characters? What choices will they be driven to? Who will they become, transmuted (to their surprise) in the fierce alchemy of your storytelling? Time to write! Go fill your story with magic! And one day, I hope I'll get to read what you create.

STANT LITORE
DECEMBER 2022

ABOUT THE AUTHOR

STANT LITORE writes about zombies, aliens, and tyrannosaurs. He does not currently own a starship or a time machine but would rather like to. He lives in Aurora, Colorado with his three children and hides from visitors in his study beneath a heap of toy dinosaurs, tattered novels, comic books, incomprehensibly scribbled drafts, and antique tomes. He has taught for Clarion West, Writing the Other, Apex Writers, and Pikes Peak Writers. He is working on his next novel, or several. You can read some of his current fiction by looking up *Ansible, The Running of the Tyrannosaurs, The Zombie Bible,* or *Dante's Heart.* However, doing so may have unpredictable effects, and Stant offers no assurances that you will emerge from any of these stories unscathed. Best leave all non-essentials behind, take with you only what you need to survive, and venture into the books cautiously and ready to call for backup. Enjoy, and good luck.

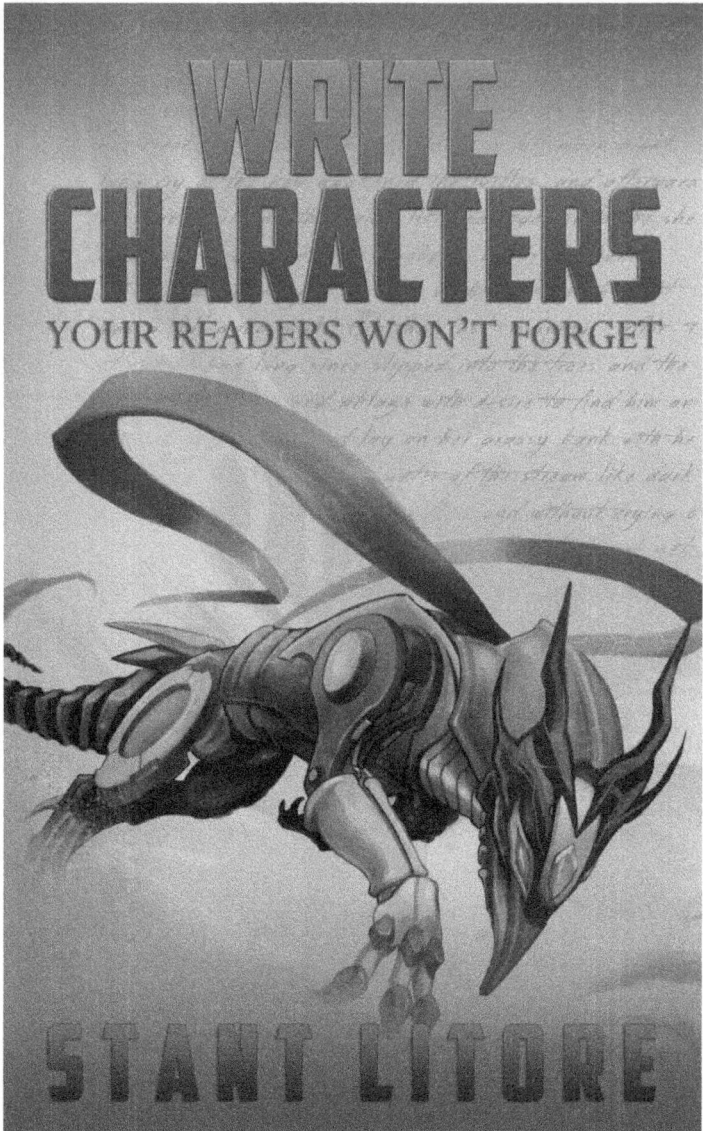

*If you enjoyed this book,
I hope you will also try:*

WRITE CHARACTERS
YOUR READERS WON'T FORGET

"I just don't care enough about your character."

Write Characters Your Readers Won't Forget is a toolkit for addressing that issue. Packed with 30 exercises, abundant examples, and practical strategies, this guidebook will help you write unforgettable characters who "come alive" on the page, create compelling dialogue, and chart more breathtaking emotional journeys for your characters.

ISBN 978-1942458050

AVAILABLE AT:

BOOKSHOP.ORG

AMAZON

BARNES & NOBLE ONLINE

STANTLITORE.COM
(direct from the author)

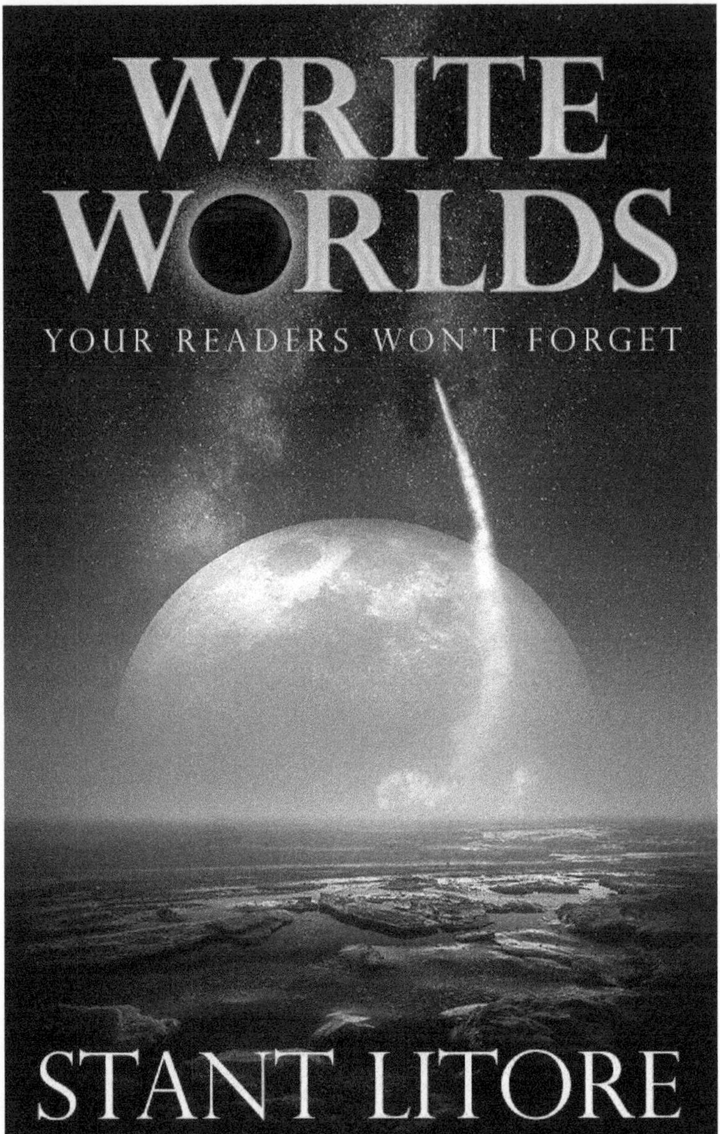
WRITE
WORLDS
YOUR READERS WON'T FORGET
STANT LITORE

WRITE WORLDS
YOUR READERS WON'T FORGET

"There are other worldbuilding books out there; this is the one you want." - Travis Heerman, author of the *Ronin* trilogy

Like a god, you get to invent a world. Maybe several. But how do you make these worlds that readers want to visit? How do you make them worlds that readers never want to leave? In *Write Worlds Your Readers Won't Forget*, explore how to create unforgettable environments, creatures, and cultures in 33 intensive exercises.

ISBN 978-1942458302

AVAILABLE AT:

BOOKSHOP.ORG

AMAZON

BARNES & NOBLE ONLINE

STANTLITORE.COM
(direct from the author)

WRITE STORIES
YOUR READERS WON'T FORGET

STANT LITORE

WRITE STORIES
YOUR READERS WON'T FORGET

"Learning to write fiction that moves readers is a lifelong pursuit, but successful writers often struggle with showing others how they do it. For that, you need a good teacher. Stant Litore is an extraordinary teacher, and in *Write Stories Your Readers Won't Forget* he shares what he knows in clear, practical and profound chapters. Packed with insight, examples, and exercises, Stant's book will cut years off your learning curve."—James Van Pelt, author of *Pandora's Gun*

Write the story you've always wanted to write. This toolkit provides a sequence of 30 story-building exercises plus guidelines on how to craft a thematic outline for your story and use it as a potent tool for revision. In these pages, explore how character, theme, and plot interact; how what matters most in your story gets expressed through each character's unique voice and gets performed dramatically through your plot; and discover how a mastery of theme can help you establish a powerful threshold text to begin your story, solve "the saggy middle," and deliver a denouement that your readers will never forget.

ISBN 978-1942458302

WRITE DESCRIPTIONS
YOUR READERS WON'T FORGET

STANT LITORE

WRITE DESCRIPTIONS
YOUR READERS WON'T FORGET

"This is the 4th book in Stant's masterclass take on writing fiction. He makes me want to rewrite everything I've done, and push onto new works. He is clear, entertaining, and passionate. I wish these books were available when I started writing, and I'm happy they are available now."—James Van Pelt, author of *Pandora's Gun*

Excite your reader on every page. Vivid description isn't a static listing of attributes; instead, it's the live wire that runs through every scene in your story, and both information and emotion travel to the reader along that hot current. It's how you make both a character's exterior world, their interior emotional life, and specific interactions between the two vivid and unforgettable. Good description is electric, and it shocks sleepy readers awake. It helps us sit up with a gasp and pay attention.

In 30 exercises, discover an entire toolkit for electrifying your prose and master fresh strategies for describing characters, settings, emotions, and actions in ways that leave the reader breathless.

ISBN 978-1736212745

WRITE
PACING
0 to 60
YOUR READERS WON'T FORGET

STANT LITORE

0 TO 60: WRITE PACING
YOUR READERS WON'T FORGET

"I'm recommending it because editors and readers often talk about the importance of pacing, but almost no one gives writers practical steps for how to effectively improve pacing—until now. I've already used several concepts from this book as I write, and I know it's one I'm going to continue to carry with me to the page."—Todd Mitchell, author of *The Last Panther* and *The Namer of Spirits*

Keep your readers on the edge of their seats. You've got great characters and a good idea for your plot, but your story builds tension too slowly; even you get bored in the middle, and you're the one writing it. How do you avoid the slow start, the overly predictable middle, the boggy subplots, and the unsatisfying ending? Pacing is not just about action. It's about the way you dance with the reader—where you drop clues, where you misdirect, where you cut between scenes, when you throw in unexpected complications, and how you raise the stakes. It's about knowing when to delay and when to deliver.

Jump into this book for Stant Litore's exhilarating crash course on pacing in fiction.

ISBN 978-1736212769

BEAT WRITER'S BLOCK

AND REIGNITE YOUR CREATIVITY

STANT LITORE

BEAT WRITER'S BLOCK AND REIGNITE YOUR CREATIVITY

Unblock your writing and recapture the playfulness of fiction.

Maybe you just can't start. Maybe you complete a first draft only to discover that it feels like a betrayal of your vision, a pale imitation of the story you had in mind. Maybe your drive toward perfection keeps you continuously editing the same scene; you just can't get it right. Maybe you don't know where your story is going anymore, or maybe you're waiting for time to get magically freed up so that you can devote long afternoons or long days to creating your story.

In this new toolkit, Stant Litore propels you through 30 exercises that will help you unblock your writing and rekindle your creativity. What we forget easily is that storytelling is play, so in this book we will recapture the excitement, play, and improvisation of fiction.

ISBN 978-1736212776